Table of Contents

Preface

I do not want anyone to believe that I am insulting another person with my skin color or if given the option, would choose to be categorized with any other group. My inclusion in the black race was initially a decision determined for me very early in life when schools made students fill out identity questionnaires on standardized tests. Apparently, this classifying was done because as a nation, we deem it necessary to statistically group our citizens, and at the time, the simple fact was that there were few choices available. Although I am a mixture of black and Asian, teachers and other authoritative adults steered everyone with my skin color and my classic features towards this choice. If someone had any dark pigmentation in their skin and a broad nose, this was the only option available.

I have since consciously chosen to maintain this categorization even after I got older and was able to arrive at my own conclusions about my racial identity. I see this identification as being sufficiently representative of my physical appearance, and since the color of my skin and most of my other physical attributes would fall under the accepted definition for inclusion in the black race, I have no problem keeping this designation. Many people today would like to describe me using numerous different race categories; nonetheless, having grown up associating myself with being a black American I feel very comfortable with this as part of my self-image. But that is all this characterization should be, a grouping of those with similar physical attributes, no different than if we had a grouping for all people with the similar eye or hair color.

Throughout our nation's history, unfortunately, these group associations have become so much more. Along with being representative of a particular set of physical attributes, American slave masters and many who followed associated personality traits, intellectual capacity, and knowledge retention capabilities, and thus, blurred the balance between genetic and environmental causal factors with respect to race. Also to our detriment, this practice has led generations of Americans to extrapolate that people specifically within the black race, because of their similar physical attributes, share the same cultural customs. We have ignored the fact that physical attributes can have negligible influence on the development of a culture or for that matter the advancement of a society or even a nation state.

I am not an anthropologist, but I believe that cultures and societies have progressed because of proximity of people rather than merely their physical characteristics bringing them together. The similar physical attributes are a result of their interaction not a cause. In our social evolution, due to limited means of transportation, people who lived close together and faced similar environmental conditions developed customs and traditions to cope with those situations specific to their locations. For instance, people located in tropical or temperate climates developed appropriate clothing, shelters, and tools which best allowed them to flourish in their surroundings. Descendents throughout time have commingled, consequently giving birth to children of like features which were best capable of adapting to these environmental conditions. The emergence of nation states and the development of better transportation have permitted many different groups to migrate and adopt the cultural customs of areas in the world which were not their original biological habitat. Currently, modern technological innovations allow people of many different races to unite and develop new customs regardless of their original points of origin. It is these cultural threads which bind groups together, more so than the areas of the world in which their physical characteristics were most adaptive.

In the relatively brief history of the United States black Americans have either migrated to this country from other homelands or were forced here on slave ships from various regions and nations of Africa. African slaves accounted for the largest proportion of blacks to enter the United States. This group of the black Americans developed a culture based on their instinct to survive during their slave beginnings. As a result, these early Americans through the natural developmental process of being in constant close proximity during their oppression and endurance of very difficult conditions at the hands of slave owners developed traditions which have manifested into the unique foods, an unyielding work ethic, and ageless art and music. This origin makes these black Americans who we will refer to for lack of a better label African Americans, unique in their ethnic foundations.

However, all black people in America, regardless of their method of migration, have been and continue to be type-casted and stereotyped and most importantly categorized, as the slave masters did, by their physical skin color. This arbitrary cataloging enables those who want to keep black Americans subservient to their culture and beliefs the ability to maintain their position of dominance. Black leaders of the past and present have accepted this characterization and tried to find strength in its unifying possibilities, but they have underestimated the resolve of those who wish to keep the black population subjugated.

The remainder of the book will examine the cultural development and repercussions of this acceptance, but now, I merely want to reiterate that I am not writing this book to imply any negative feelings towards any individuals in my race. In this book, I am stating that there must be changes in understanding in order for everyone to see the reality which black Americans already know. Simply, just as among white Americans, there are cultural differences between black Americans which make their experiences unique and group specific. Furthermore, I believe we are at a moment in our history where perpetuating this stereotyping will have more negative effects on our future generations than the positive outcomes which may result from blacks unifying against continued discrimination. In addition, we are all guilty of passing on the slave masters' doctrine; therefore, I am not accusing any particular group or person. My message is for us to look within and forward, so our children may be seen through the prism of their individual identities, and as such be appreciated as stated by Reverend Dr. Martin Luther King, Jr. in his "*I have a Dream*" speech for *the content of their character, not be judged by the color of their skin.*

Dedicate this book to Samantha and Madison;
I hope this book changes how they are viewed.
I would also like to thank all those who took the time to
give me their opinions and suggestions.

Introduction

While raising my two daughters, I recognized the lack of knowledge most people possess with respect to race, ethnicity, and nationality issues. My daughters' ethnicity is one quarter Dutch, one quarter German and half Jamaican, and their race description is half white, one quarter Asian and one quarter black. These ethnic mixtures throughout our history caused a great deal of misunderstandings due to their complexities and social ramifications. Our intermixing produced a rich blending of the American *melting pot*. As a result, history demonstrates that this creation is ultimately the primary source of strength for the United States. This amazing diversity gives America a singular position in the world, where our nation stands alone as the beacon of light, illuminating an oasis in which all inhabitants of the world can live together in harmony. Nationalities that war with each other in their native lands come to our shores and live together as neighbors in the same communities; for example, only in America do Israelis live peacefully with Saudis, and Frenchmen live happily near Italians.

The ability of our citizens to live in unity is a testimony to the greatness of the system devised by our forefathers. It is plainly the most extraordinary system ever conceived by man. The Constitution allows for the assimilation of all groups who are willing to accept the values and principles of the United States. They can prosper and thrive like nowhere else on earth. The document is exceptionally rigid and flexible at the same time, enabling changes, but not making them too easy so that they have no meaning. The majority of citizens cannot run roughshod over the minority citizen groups, because our founding fathers recognized that the will of the majority should not always be the law of the land; the rights of the minority ought to be protected regardless of the determination of the majority. Above all else, no person shall be encumbered from their pursuit of happiness, stopped from enjoying their life, and not permitted to exercise their liberty. Our founding fathers constructed a nation that is not dependent on the achievements of one group, but encourages the harmonious commingling of all ethnic nationalities. They acknowledged the *"perfect union"* and structured the system to best achieve the ideal, without sacrificing the integrity of the institutions, even if the pinnacle is not attained.

The most pervasive exception to this seemingly well construed system is the plight of black Americans. Over my life, I am a firsthand witness to the discrimination and segregation which is suffered by many blacks in America. This treatment has incredibly strong underpinnings in all regions of our nation. The perpetrators of this behavior have and continue to exist since our nation's inception. But most of the conduct was focused on a particular group of black Americans, namely African Americans. The incomprehensible treatment of African Americans was unparalleled in its brutality and barbarism. Other ethnic groups have experienced discrimination and isolation, like the Japanese

13

and the Irish, but no group has had to endure the unrelenting demeaning and deplorable conditions which have been experienced by African Americans. The barbaric activities have spilled over to all black Americans and even many other citizens of color, representing the most egregious contradiction to our founding fathers' original intentions.

In my twenties, I simply could not understand why the roots of discrimination ran so deep, and the angry wounds of hatred towards black Americans were so long-lasting and bleeding so profusely, with many lesions showing no possibility of healing. As I investigated the history of blacks in America, I realized that America continues both overtly and inadvertently to treat blacks in similar ways as the slave masters had in the past. One blatant example is that America, in spite of modern day correctness, still considers anyone with any black pedigree to be solely black. With my daughters having just a small percentage of black lineage, I believe it is wrong for slave masters to continue dictating and determining their classification. It should be up to them who they want to be and how they wish to be perceived by others. Furthermore, because of the subconscious and covert bias which is present in society as a result of the large grouping, my children will never be judged by their character if we do not insist that they are treated like individuals first.

Additionally, a friend studying social work showed me articles about social scientists searching for a *"black culture"* which is representative of all black people. It had always been obvious to me that all black people were not the same culturally, and I thought this was common knowledge to everyone, because all my friends and relatives knew that there are obvious differences between different black groups. This idea of a *black culture* is ridiculous, because even black people from the same country in Africa may have completely different cultures. Africa consists of thousands of different tribal regions, which follow very different customs and traditions. Needless to say, the many other nations of the world where black people come from have countless different cultures.

I was shocked to realize that many Americans do believe that all blacks should be familiar with each other, and we all have the same cultural genesis. For instance, many people I have met thought I should know what Kwanzaa was, and of course, assumed I celebrated it. I would say to them, "*Are you knowledgeable with respect to all white traditions or share the same white culture?*" From their blank expressions, I knew I did not want my daughters growing up in a country that did not have a clue about the different ethnic groups that makes this nation so great. Also, I wanted everyone to know the true history of those blacks who were forced to come to America, and that they should be recognized as a specific ethnic group labeled African Americans, and like other cultures, include people of different races, particularly whites, who are hiding from this heritage. Other blacks, like me, who migrated from different places, do not have the same cultural origins as African Americans whom came via the slave trade, and certainly we do not have the same past. African American history is distinctive and should be studied separately, because only through individual case examination shall the issues which surround their situation be understood and overcome.

The development of this book illustrates a personal quest into my own identity, journaling my progression of knowledge with respect to the black experience in America. It shows the information I tried to learn about the history of slavery, battles of the civil rights movement, and consistent perseverance of blacks to succeed, especially African Americans. The chapters expound upon the *Who, Where, What, When, How*, and *Why* questions I pondered during my journey, focusing on those individuals who I perceived have changed how black Americans are viewed, particular, Dr. Martin Luther King, Jr., whose life exemplifies how we all can strive for the *mountaintop*. I found the lifelong struggles of certain key historical figures to be paramount to my understanding and the growth of my awareness. I realize that this is by no means a complete history or a full account of where blacks have come or the challenges which remain in the future, but this information gave me a better knowledge and broader perspective of all the topics involved, allowing me to better identify who I am. If this trek encourages someone to pursue their own personal level of realization, then I am rewarded for my efforts.

As an aside, during the researching of this book it has been very difficult to find information which ethnically differentiates the various groups of black Americans from African Americans. Over a century later, slave masters still dictate how we collect information. As a result, it was almost impossible to keep the usage of certain terminology consistent. Although I tried my best, there are places in the book where some confusion may arise, where black and African American are unavoidably used interchangeably. I, however, want to emphasize that I recognize that African Americans comprise the majority of black Americans, so most of the statistics which are quoted throughout, though may be influenced by other blacks, probably are not significantly different from numbers that would be reported if African Americans were the only respondents. Moreover, in simplistic terms, most African Americans are black; however, not all blacks are African Americans. In the same way, most Italian Americans are white, but not all whites are Italian Americans. Always keep this in mind.

Who are black Americans?

By stating that I do not consider myself African American, indicates that I believe that my cultural and ethnic heritage would be better described in other terms. In my opinion, the more accurate description is Jamaican American. I was born in Jamaica and came to this country legally when I was 4 years old. My mother and I remained *"in line"* for two years, waiting for our visa number to be chosen from the thousands of Jamaicans applying for access to the United States. Meantime, my father, who left Jamaica years earlier, worked and prepared for our arrival. He pledged to have the means to support us when we finally were granted approval. After living here as a resident alien for the required seven years, I became a naturalized citizen. My story is very similar to millions of Americans who came to the United States to seek a better life and achieve the *American Dream.*

Due to no fault of their own, African Americans were not given this choice. This basic fact alone makes Jamaican Americans and African Americans different, but I recognized further distinctions early in my life. Many would ask, *"What is the difference?"* to which I would facetiously answer, *"What is the difference between a Frenchman and an Italian?"* Those who say nothing do not know any Frenchmen or Italians. It was seemingly easy for everyone to see the differences between the many white ethnicities, but with respect to black people we were all seen as the same with no differentiation. As a result, our individuality was lost, and the uniqueness of each ethnic group and its impact on American society was minimized. As a side note, this must have given rise to the saying, *"They all look the same to us."*

It is true that Jamaica was on the slave trade route and many of the black Jamaicans were originally from slave ships; however, that is where the similarities end. The cultural development which followed the slaves who were brought to America and the slaves who were left on the island of Jamaica were very different. The indignities of the American slaves at the hands of the Southern slave masters were deplorable and demeaning. The African slaves which were left to inhabit Jamaica, although they did not immediately find equality or freedom, were left in a much less dreadful situation. Slavery was outlawed in the British colonies in 1833, and practically speaking, the British were *absentee* slave masters. When the British ended slavery they immediately made ex-slaves citizens of the Empire, and created an equal school system which would educate the entire population. As a result, blacks were relatively quickly assimilated into Jamaican life and culture.

Of course, this does not mean there was no prejudice against blacks in Jamaica; unfortunately, there was prejudice between the different races on the island. But the English, who governed the island for most of its history, were able to put all minority races in their place while stripping Jamaica of many of its inherently valuable treasures. After gaining its independence

19

in 1962, Jamaica became a country of numerous conflicting races and ethnicities. Consequently, when all factions have very little of tangible value and an unwillingness to cooperate with each other, it does not matter which group assumes power. Their reign over other groups is short lived and the people of every faction are left discouraged by the constant transitioning, leaving a nation with a continuously unstable governmental system, little wealth and many needlessly suffering in poverty. Though the citizens coveted the beauty of their island, their dreams and hopes were tied to waiting for an opportunity to come to America and follow their economic aspirations.

Nevertheless, many people ask me why do I not consider myself African American, are not all black Americans, African Americans? This widely held belief is the root of the problem. Being African American has become synonymous with being black, and this is a false relationship. African American is not the sole ethnicity of all black Americans. If the label African American was used properly, it would be the description of a particular group of black Americans describing their ethnicity or cultural heritage and not their race. Ethnicity refers to someone's place of origin and cultural identity, and race is used to group humans of like genetic characteristics. For instance, the term Italian American refers to someone from Italy and who is an American citizen, not necessarily a white person. As a matter of fact, I have met quite a few dark skin Italians. I understand the reason why this relationship between the two terms has developed, but we have to discontinue using the terms incorrectly. This inaccurate usage is distracting us from being able to properly identify and correct the problems which are plaguing the individual ethnic communities, especially the African American. Social scientists and social workers are looking for a *"black culture"* which does not exist. They hope to use this knowledge to determine cures for this seemingly *faulty cultural system.* Fruitless excursions like this into a false belief only mask the true path to real change in a community. In addition, although African Americans do account for the vast majority of blacks in America, this global characterization is allowing those who would continue to demean and denigrate black people the avenue to do so, with bogus diagnoses such as *black rage, black anti-intellectualism,* and *black victimology.*

There is an African American culture, which has fostered incredible foods, given birth to amazing music and art, and changed American life, forever. However, even those who originally descended from this heritage have been assimilated into different cultures due to the areas in the country where they eventually migrated. Black Americans are a culturally diverse group with African American being merely one of the ethnicities. African American is an ethnic group which grew from the plantations and homesteads of the South, as a result of slavery. The label African American was coined in order to provide people who are descendents of these slaves a place of origin, which is similar to the other immigrant groups who have come to America.

21

For example, Polish Americans, Irish Americans and Chinese Americans are all descriptions referring to the place of origin of a certain ethnic group. The obvious problem with the origin of slaves was that no records were kept documenting the exact origins of any individual slave. Thus, it is impossible to trace a slave back to any particular country in Africa. Moreover, slave masters kept very few birth records and intentionally broke up families in order to weaken the family bonds, which they believed gave them more control over their property. Therefore, descendents of these slaves are left searching in vain for their points of origin. As a result, the genealogy of their descendents is incomplete; affecting how they see themselves and also how others identify them.

Another consequence of this incorrect alignment is the lack of identification of white African Americans. Just like there are white Jamaican Americans, there should be white African Americans. Throughout the history of America, there have been relationships between slaves and their masters which have been hidden in the genealogy of many families. Also, there were relationships between African American men and European American women resulting in offspring that were tucked away in the dark corners of some family trees. The descendents of these relationships should also be included when referring to African Americans. They continue many of the same cultural traditions as other African Americans and have some of the same problems with identity and self-esteem. This more encompassing group would allow a much larger segment of the population to come together and attack the issues which face African Americans. Additionally, someone could not discriminate so easily against another person if he thought that person was their fellow ethnic group member.

I am in no way proclaiming that Jamaican Americans do not have problems assimilating into American society or that we do not have inherent issues which plague our community. We face many problems which inhibit our advancement; however, our concerns are faced by almost every immigrant group that has come to America. In addition, our inherently Jamaican difficulties could also be better identified if they were viewed through the prism of our particular cultural development. Nonetheless, like all immigrant groups we come to America knowing that we leave behind a desperately worse situation, with much less opportunity, so we arrive motivated to find our *American Dream*. We recognize that there is no going back from where we came, not because we cannot, but merely because our emigration to America was a "*succeed at all cost or die trying*" proposition. Going back to our countries of origin without attaining our *American Dream* was never an option. Like all immigrants, our view of the greatness of America is seen relative to the inadequacies of our countries of origin. As a result, we always must maintain the optimism with respect to our ability to be successful rather than focus on the daunting obstacles which may inhibit our path.

African Americans had no choice in coming to this land, which has resulted in numerous scars on their collective psyche. Slave masters took away an African American's point of reference, literally ripping them from their places of origin, which makes their experience inimitable with respect to every other ethnic group that has come to the American shores. Even the earliest pilgrims who settled this new land came from a place which treated them much worse than any obstacles they encountered in the new world. African Americans do not have this point of reference, and as a consequence of the systematic and pervasive oppression they have received; first, at the hands of the slave masters and then through the many years of inaction and persecution by their fellow citizens of the United States, African Americans must collectively view America not as the land of opportunity, but as the country which refuses to give them a fair chance. However, as their history indicates, African Americans have been one of the most patriotic ethnic groups every to come to America, willing to defend their country whenever duty calls.

Fellow Jamaican, Marcus Garvey, founder of United Negro Improvement Association, at the beginning of the 20th century spoke and wrote extensively about this lack of choice of American black people. He at the time in many speeches and editorials championed the establishment of a black nation. Although I completely disagree with his concept because America has the capacity to incorporate all groups into its melting pot, Marcus Garvey was one of the first to highlight the need for

24

cultural identity which would build cohesion between American blacks and black people around the world. He was unable to convince other black organizations, such as the National Association for the Advancement of Colored People (NAACP) led by William Edward Burghardt "W.E.B" Du Bois, because the black race did not have a common culture or similar view of the future. The NAACP viewed Garvey as *"without doubt, the most dangerous enemy of the Negro race in America."*

This reality is, of course, neither an excuse nor a justification for the treatment and condition of black Americans, particularly African Americans. It is, simply, a frame of understanding which should provide some illumination to the problems in the different black American communities. Specifically, America has for too long camouflaged the concerns in the African American population by comparing them with the problems of other immigrant Americans; thus, failing to achieve any real understanding of the issues which afflict this particular ethnic group, leaving solutions which would be applicable to this group of citizens to remain elusive. As a nation, our leaders only respond to the effects of these underlying issues by asking accusatory questions as to why African American neighborhoods have not thrived like other ethnic residents who immigrated to America. Therefore, we simply perpetuate the degradation of the African American culture and families which was initiated by slave masters; hence, allowing slave masters' preaching and dogma to survive unchallenged in many areas of American society.

As I stated earlier, I recognized the dissimilarities between Jamaicans and African Americans at a young age. Jamaica, being one of the colonies of Great Britain for much of its history, derived most of its customs, traditions, and basic structure from British colonial societies, so they closely mirrored European traditions. These similarities to Europeans made it easier for me to relate to Americans of European descent than it was for me to interact with African Americans. I always found this inclination very perplexing, resulting in isolation and some dissociation. Many African American students resented me for my preference to associate with children of European descent. At first this caused me great anxiety until I began to understand why I had a better sense of belonging in a group of white students than in a group of fellow black students.

Because of my family's cultural experiences, we celebrated and practiced our traditional holiday ceremonies and our religious services more closely mimicking long-established European rituals rather than customary African American conventions. It was very easy for me to make friends with many different white Americans and attend their parties and family occasions because they were more analogous to my own family events. My family also felt extremely comfortable attending predominantly white churches because their preaching was like the religious services we were accustomed to in Jamaica. It was not till later in my life that I was able to appreciate the liveliness and vivacious atmosphere of an African American Baptist service.

With all this being said, I still cannot succinctly define the ethnicities of all black Americans, because it is impossible to completely encapsulate an entire populations' ethnic groupings. Even when a certain people may have the same place of origin, their cultural traditions can vary greatly. For example, Indian Americans, who originated from India, their culture and rituals can be vastly different because of the influence of the religion they follow, whether it be Hindu, Muslim, Christianity, or Buddhism. In general, an ethnicity can incorporate many different races and many religious traditions; accordingly, making it very difficult to discriminate against individuals with a particular ethnic background, although many people do try. However, it is easy to define someone's race due to the fact it is based on many visible physical attributes, mainly someone's skin color. This simplistic definition has allowed the legacy of slave masters to continue for more than 150 years after President Lincoln's *Emancipation Proclamation*, oppressing anyone with black skin, and by our tendency to equate African American with being black and believing this ethnic grouping is the only one which identifies black Americans, this domination can continue well into our future.

Where did black Americans originate?

The label, *African American*, is only the latest description of black Americans. This moniker continued the ongoing process of grouping all black Americans together; though unfortunately, it also strengthened the effort of eliminating the individuality of blacks. This practice started with the first Africans who were forced to come to America via slave ships starting in the 17th century. *Negro* was the oldest identifier used by the slave masters in the early days of the slave trade. Other descriptions were adopted by southerners throughout American history such as *coloreds, Blacks* and *Nigger*. *Nigger* was first used by the slave masters synonymously with Negro to designate black slaves. It was not until later in our history that *Nigger* became a pejorative term identifying a slow dull witted black person. Presently, many black Americans use *Nigga* as a term of endearment in order to diminish *Nigger's* negative connotation.

During the 50's and 60's with the rise of the civil rights movement, the leaders, specifically Malcolm X, started trying to find labels that would better unify and strengthen the movement while creating a cultural identity for the black race. Malcolm X conceived names such *Afro-American* and *Black African*. Other leaders through history have referred to blacks using many different terms, but in his presidential campaign of 1988 in an effort to mobilize the black population, Jesse Jackson popularized

African American finally making it the accepted brand of the black American leadership.

This label was able to provide a place of origin which solved one of the missing identity issues that plagued the descendents of black African slaves. In addition, it equated the *black slave experience* with the many other immigrant groups, which have so successfully assimilated into American society; somewhat, trying to erase the stigma associated with the long history of oppression and persecution suffered by black Americans. Regardless of the intentions of this label, the slave beginnings make the African American evolutionary progression singular among all other ethnicities.

From my very earliest understanding of the slave trade in America, it was clear that slavery was completely contradictory to every value which our founding fathers expounded as the cornerstones of our union. Although inexcusable, I can see through the prism of our modern day politics why they could not from the very start of our country eliminate the existence of slavery. With such a large percentage of our national population believing in the validity of slavery, it would have been impossible to form our union and revolt against the British if the founding fathers tried to address the slavery issue simultaneously. They calculatedly left the inevitable war over the issue of slavery for another day. Nevertheless, those who were enslaved were left to endure another eighty or so years of simply deplorable treatment and conditions. Even the few Negroes who were able to gain their freedom and come to the northern states which had abolished slavery were treated as low class non-citizens, with few rights and privileges. Hence, few were innocent from perpetuating the discrimination and exploitation which was experienced by the Negro population.

Though there were many founders from the very first days of our nation who knew that the continued expansion of the slave economy was in direct conflict with the principles for which the Constitution was based, of the founding fathers, George Washington was the only southern plantation owner to take the action of ordering his slaves emancipated upon the death of his widow. Martha Washington, to her credit, did not wait to initiate the release of her slaves until her own death; although a slave owner most of her life, she began emancipating her slaves just 12 months following the death of our first President in 1799. Northerners, such as Benjamin Franklin and John Jay, began the process of freeing their slaves upon the end of the Revolutionary War.

In contrast to his apparent personal beliefs, George Washington, as President, signed one of the first national legislations into law which was meant to further appease the southern slave owners and proclaim black people as property with no human rights. In 1793, he signed the Fugitive Slave Law which gave slave owners the right to recapture their fugitive slaves even in the northern states that had abolished slavery. He also appropriated $400,000, thousands of weapons and emergency supplies to aid the slave owners in what is now called Haiti to squash the slave rebellion of 1794. Additionally, even earlier, Washington signed the <u>Naturalization Act</u> in 1790 which enabled free white people who immigrated to the United States to become citizens, later establishing the Caucasian classification as a litmus test for citizenship.

Furthermore, when ratifying the Constitution, founders such as Alexander Hamilton, who spoke openly about his opposition to slavery and for whom many biographers have hailed as an abolitionist, defended in *The Federalists' Papers* giving southern slave states unwarranted over representation in Congress. This provision allowed pro-slavery supporters to dominate the national debate on slavery and pass legislation with the intention of enhancing their slave agenda. Article 1, Section 2, Paragraph 3 of the United States Constitution, the <u>Three Fifth Compromise</u> allowed southern states to count their slave population as three fifths of a citizen for the purpose of tax allocation and representation in the House of Representatives. This Compromise authored by James Madison enticed the southern slave states to ratify the Constitution. As a consequence, it led to years of slave based legislation which allowed slave states to not only grow their slave economies but also reach into new territories; it enabled slave masters to pass additional inhumane laws which worsened the living conditions of slave families leading to the destruction of the slave family unit for generations to follow. Moreover, the Constitution in Article 1, Section 9, Clause 1, forbade Congress from outlawing slavery until 1808, at which time, the Congress still did not outlaw slavery. In another compromise, Congress merely made it illegal to import any additional slaves from Africa.

As a result of these constitutional provisions, the years following the birth of our nation witnessed a growth in slave legislation, both on the state and federal levels of government. Although many of the prominent leaders condemned slavery, the legislative power given to the slave states in order to bring the country together resulted in policies that were contradictory to the principles for which the founders advocated. One of the states at the forefront of these active slave based legislative agendas was Virginia, the home of two of our most important founding fathers, George Washington and Thomas Jefferson. After George Washington in his will emancipated his own slaves, the Virginia legislature passed laws in order to make it more difficult to free slaves upon someone's death. As a result, Thomas Jefferson was unable to emancipate any of his slaves. Alan Axelrod, Ph.D. wrote in his biography of Thomas Jefferson, <u>The Life and Work of Thomas Jefferson</u> that "*Even if Jefferson had wanted to emancipate his slaves immediately, Virginia law would not have let him do so, at least not easily. If a Virginia slave owner wanted to free a slave, he had to prove in court a basis of 'meritorious service' on the part of the slave.*"

Virginia and other southern states also passed additional laws which strengthened the position of slave masters, and kept the Negroes in a subservient position, thus, allowing the perpetuation of the slave economy. The demand for slavery amplified greatly after Eli Whitney created the Cotton Gin in 1793. The price of slaves inflated dramatically. The possible profits in the cotton industry due to more production increased greatly, causing state legislatures to institute more slavery friendly laws in order to keep the dollars flowing.

Most tragically, these laws purposefully destroyed the family unit of Negroes by keeping the fathers away from their children. One of those laws passed in 1799 was instituted in Virginia in order to deal with mulatto children of white mothers, banishing them and their children from the Virginian territory. Despite the fact that these children were supposed to be free because slavery was deemed to be dependent on the status of one's mother, resulting from a Virginia Law passed in 1662, which stated that the *law of hereditary slavery meant that a child born to an enslaved mother inherits her slave status.* Another attack on the family unit were laws passed in Louisiana, South Carolina and other southern states which did not allow for the recognition of marriage between slaves; in fact, marriage was strictly forbidden. Slave families were seen as an impediment to the advancement of slavery and the slave economy.

After the slave plot organized by Gabriel Prosser, an enslaved blacksmith, to kill white people in Virginia was foiled in 1800, Virginia passed more laws to stop the congregation of blacks for the purpose of gaining religious knowledge or for any purpose which in any way enhanced their education. This period was considered the *Second Great Awakening* because during this period there was a strong push to convert slaves to Christianity in large numbers. Religious leaders believed it was the will of God to enlighten these savage Africans to teachings of the Lord. However, Gabriel Prosser, who saw himself as being directed by God, like Moses, used these religious meetings to organize his revolt instead. Further, in 1819 Virginia went and joined other southern states in outlawing the education of blacks by anyone, whether in a group or individually. No one was allowed to teach a black person, whether free or slave, to read and write. Slave masters wanted nothing especially education to stand in the way of their flourishing slave industry, and the earnings which were generated from both the trading of slaves and the crops that were produced by their labor.

In particular, the invention of the cotton gin enhanced the profitability and productivity of slaves, and substantial grew the wealth of slave masters. As such they looked to the west for expansion of their agricultural economy. The federal government and the northern non-slave states fought hard to keep slavery out of the western territories. After the Louisiana Purchase, the Missouri Compromise was passed in 1820 which made all territories north of the southern border of Missouri non-slave territory. The Compromise also allowed the incorporation of Maine as a non slave state with the inclusion of Missouri as a slave state. The battle over the growth of the southern economy had begun. This ideological difference over the extension of the southern agrarian economy and the resulting need for the expansion of slavery would lead to the eventual Civil War.

In the years leading up to the war, southern states held steadfast to their economic need to maintain slavery. They passed further laws aimed at silencing the ever growing number of slave revolts and the increasingly louder voices of the northern abolitionist. In 1831, Virginia passed a law prohibiting the congregation of blacks for religious services anywhere, regardless if the service was being performed by a black or white preacher. Also, the House of Representatives consisting of an over represented southern contingent and faced with inundation of abolitionists' petitions calling for the emancipation of slaves, voted to automatically table the petitions upon arrival. Basically, the petitions were immediately discarded without any consideration. These avoidance measures were only temporary band aids on the ever enlarging open wound which was growing throughout the union. Slavery was ripping the nation apart, both in Congress and in every state in the country.

As in the <u>Missouri Compromise</u>, every time a non-slave state was let into the Union the southern states insisted on the inclusion of a slave state, so by 1850 with the admittance of California as a non slave state came the inclusion of New Mexico and Utah as slave states. Hence, as the country grew, so did slavery. Many abolitionists could no longer tolerate this continued expansion. Abolitionist John Brown became violent after an attack on Lawrence, Kansas by a proslavery group.

Brown led retaliation against the assailants, but then continued to lead violent attacks throughout the south in an attempt to disrupt the slave trade. Finally, when Abraham Lincoln, an abolitionist, was elected President, the South formed the Union of Confederate States and elected their own President, Jefferson Davis. With this declaration, the Civil War was underway and 75,000 black soldiers immediately ran to join the Union army and fight for their freedom, but they were rejected, not allowed to fight for their own freedom. About a year later the Union army realized the need for these able bodied soldiers and created black divisions. The black soldiers were vital to the northern victory, and the emancipated black people relished their new acquired liberty.

After 1863, when President Abraham Lincoln issued the Emancipation Proclamation, freeing all slaves in the country, and the Thirteenth Amendment of the Constitution abolishing slavery throughout the country went into law in1865 at the end of the Civil War, blacks were led to believe that this new freedom would enable them to live without any barriers impeding their pursuit of happiness. They were promised the same opportunities as anyone else to succeed in this new free America. However, the northern lawmakers in Congress now wanted to punish the southern states for seceding from the Union and were going to use this newly emancipated black constituency as a tool for inflicting their retribution. This period is called the "*Radical Reconstruction*." After Lincoln was shot and President Andrew Johnson, a democrat, assumed the presidency, Congress led by northern republicans overrode his more moderate approach to the reconstruction of the southern governments in order to institute their more vindictive approach. The Congress gave blacks voting rights while limiting the rights of Confederate whites, so that republicans using Negro politicians could take control of these outlaw state governments, basically creating federal military districts overseen by the Union army.

South Carolina in 1868 became the only state legislature in the history of the United States that consisted of a black majority. This approach thoroughly infuriated the white southerners leading to the formation of radical white supremacy groups such as the Ku Klux Klan. The Klan's sole purpose was to eradicate the *black plague* that was in their view, imposing on their rights. Membership in the Klan was very high among these angry white southerners, and they specialized in covert operations of intimidation and violence. Consequently, the southern states after readmission into the union were able to form *Redeemer* governments which democratically elected legislatures that were whites only. Through intimidation, poll taxes and literacy requirements, this oppressive form of government was able to take over all southern states and blacks were essentially forcefully pushed out of the political arena, as the federal government withdrew union troops and reconstruction came to an end. The northern republicans lost their majority in Congress and the southern democrats took over leaving blacks with no further allies in the federal government, and only the angry southerners left to control their fate.

By 1881 with white supremacy reestablished and *Redeemer* governments in all southern states, Tennessee became the first state to pass *Jim Crow* laws, segregating the state railroad and all other state institutions. *Jim Crow* was a character from a song of the same name which became a derogatory reference to black people, similar to *Nigger*. Almost immediately all southern states started passing laws which would relegate black people to second class citizens by keeping the white population and the black population separated. These laws stayed in existence until the late 1960's demonstrating just how angry the white southerners were over this brief period of blacks being used by northerners to control southern states, and how powerless the black population has remained, as a result.

As a side note, if President Lincoln had not been shot on that terrible night at the Ford Theater, black people might not have endured such abuse over the last 100 years, President Lincoln along with Vice President Johnson had a moderate view of reconstruction. President Lincoln, being a republican, could have controlled the overzealous republican congress, making reconstruction much less of a vengeful experience. President Lincoln's reconstruction plan called for only ten percent of the state population to take a loyalty oath, and in turn the southern leaders would receive amnesty from all war activities. This plan might have placed blacks in a much better position even if they would have received fewer rights initially. Blacks would have surely accepted fewer liberties in the short run for a more natural assimilation into the American society. Of course, this is only speculation.

Additionally, the nation through Supreme Court ruling officially adopted the slave master's definition of a black person, meaning, that any black blood in someone's heritage automatically categorized that person as black. Therefore, anyone who looked white, but knowingly had a black heritage would hide their black genealogy or suffer the degradation of their fellow black citizens. In the case, *Plessy vs. Ferguson* in 1896, the Supreme Court not only upheld the legality of segregation on the basis of "*separate but equal*," it legitimately established the precedent that any amount of black blood made someone black. Homer Plessy, who was predominately white with only one eighth black heritage, was made to sit in the black only cars on the Louisiana railroad. The significance of this case was validation of the resulting isolation of all black people. Although it was implicitly understood before, this case marked the moment in history where the black race became a "*black cultural*" group. Hence, this false definition of *black* continues to be used in our present day discussions.

The next eighty years for blacks were marred with incredible challenges, both personal and societal. Most blacks had to face these persistent segregation laws which daily degraded their personal self-worth, such as being seated on the back of buses, in the kitchen at restaurants, if the restaurant would even serve them, and in the baggage cars on trains. But these personal indignations were nothing compared to the societal economic setbacks which blacks were made to endure. Employment opportunities were limited for blacks because white business owners would only allow black people to perform certain jobs, and even in those menial jobs they were paid less than their white counterparts. This obviously did not enable black people to have the same upward mobility as white families, making it difficult for them to pull themselves out of poverty. Moreover, the majority of blacks lived in the rural south where job opportunities were scarce. Most blacks ended up working on parcels of land which were rented to them by white land owners and payment for these farms consisted of the majority of the harvest which was reaped from the land, so most black families could do no better than barely feed their families with the remainder of the yield. For many blacks the only way out, as during slavery, was to escape to the big cities in the north and try to achieve their *American Dream*.

Black Leaders, like Booker T. Washington, emerged and began emphasizing the need for education and economic advancement as the means by which blacks would overcome segregation. Washington founded the Tuskegee Institute which was the state college for blacks in Alabama. In his famous agreement called the *Atlanta Compromise*, Washington promised white civic leaders that black leaders would encourage the masses to avoid confrontation over segregation. Instead he pledged to encourage Negroes to invest their energies into education; in return white business leaders would provide them with economic opportunities throughout Georgia, along with decent facilities to house black only schools. Booker T. Washington's moderate viewpoint made him a favorite of many in the elite white community. He was the adviser to both President Theodore Roosevelt and President William Taft. After President Roosevelt read Washington's second biography, *Up from Slavery*, he made Washington the first black American to be invited to the White House for dinner. As an example that attitudes throughout the South were not changing any time soon, South Carolina Senator Benjamin Tillman commented after hearing about the dinner, *"The action of President Roosevelt in entertaining that nigger will necessitate our killing a thousand niggers in the South before they learn their place again."*

More radical leaders also rose out of the poverty and despair that characterized most Negroes' lives. W.E.B Du Bois, one of the founders of the NAACP, was the first Negro to graduate from Harvard University with a Doctorate. Du Bois released the *Niagara Movement* which was a collection of writings that outlined principles contradicting those articulated by Booker T. Washington in the *Atlanta Compromise*. He felt that Washington gave up the Negro *"manhood"* in order to gain a few menial jobs and some dilapidated educational facilities. Du Bois led Negroes away from the Republican Party after President

Roosevelt dishonorably discharged 167 black soldiers for their alleged "*conspiracy of silence*" in the *Brownsville Affair*. In this incident, town officials insisted that black soldiers were responsible for shooting two white men in Brownsville, Texas. One victim was dead and the other was wounded. Although Fort Brown commanders accounted for all black infantrymen, President Roosevelt on fictitious evidence and without any trial or due process dismissed the soldiers without honor. Booker T. Washington tried to quietly get the President to reverse his decision, but Roosevelt was steadfast in his actions. Finally in 1972, after a thorough investigation these soldiers were given back their military rankings and the benefits for which they were entitled.

Du Bois was furious with President Roosevelt and Booker T. Washington. Consequently, he made a deal with democrat Woodrow Wilson to endorse him for president in the next election. In exchange, Wilson promised to focus on issues which were important to the Negro population. It turned out that President Wilson was extremely racist and did nothing to improve the predicament of Negroes. He actually imposed further segregation on black federal employees, which had been previously integrated for the last 50 years.

Negroes were merely used to help one party defeat the other, in this case, Wilson defeat Taft, and again, when their purpose was fulfilled they were discarded and forgotten, tossed aside as if their lives had no value. Both political parties continued to treat the Negro vote like it was disposable, but the frustration in the black communities throughout the nation was reaching a fevered pitch. When Negroes no longer could stand all the injustices that continued to plague their people, they would rise up and riot in an attempt to have their voices heard. However, this fever usually resulted in the blacks protesting for their rights, and whites killing them as if they were animals. The preposterous outcome of these uprisings was that the blacks were always the ones arrested and convicted for the murders and destruction of property which occurred to themselves and their neighborhoods, with very few positive results to show for their fervor.

Furthermore, another victimized group who considered blacks to be the reason for their troubles was low income whites; as a result, they resented any blacks who had a better life than they had achieved. The Tulsa Race Riots marked such a moment when resentment bubbled out of control. Eight hundred white low income males attacked an upscale black neighborhood in Tulsa, Oklahoma, considered one of the richest black neighborhoods in the country, and destroyed all the homes in the area, while killing unofficially 300 black people. The police arrested 6,000 Negroes, some for their own safety, but most for causing the damage to their own homes and killing their neighbors. The riot left 10,000 blacks homeless throughout Tulsa, and not a single white person was arrested for this vicious, unprovoked attack. Frankly, it really did not matter what Negroes worked for or accomplished; whites could at any moment take it all away without any retribution for their actions.

The beginning of World War I found Negroes ready to fight once more for their country, but their country was not ready to have black people on the battle fields. Subsequently, very few Negro soldiers were allowed to fight in actual combat. The military commanders categorized Negro soldiers as inferior to white soldiers, because they had preconceived notions that blacks were not as smart or as disciplined as their white counterparts. Along with their prejudices, these conclusions were further reinforced by faulty information perpetuated by unfit commanders. The War Department hired outside consultants to determine the best formula for training Negro soldiers. After presentation of the consultation reports, commanders realized that these determinations were based on terrible training methods and inadequate leadership. As the war continued and the need for more soldiers was apparent, the Army deduced from the recommendations that these black battalions could be better prepared and play a bigger role in the war if they were led by Negro officers. Therefore, the Army opened a black officer training school at Fort Des Moines, but after the first graduating class the Army shut down the school. The Army decided to use established training facilities or special training camps in other areas of the country, which already were training white officers. This new approach enabled black officers to train alongside their white counterparts. The Army was leading the nation towards an integrated population.

The War Department also realized that it was impossible to get enough troops through the voluntary system so they had to institute selective service for males 21 to 31. Draft boards were established all over the country to enlist local candidates. Negroes actually faced a reversed discrimination, where draft boards would place them on the top of the list before eligible white candidates. Negro males who were sole providers to their families on their farms would be chosen before single white factory workers. Ironically, Negroes, even when they are put on the top of the list, were forced to suffer from injustice in some fashion.

The conditions for most Negro soldiers were reportedly horrible throughout different branches of the military. There were reports of Negro soldiers having to sleep outside in tents when separate barracks could not be constructed. Those black soldiers also had to eat outside where mess halls facilities were not available. This treatment continued regardless of the weather conditions outside. Negroes also were clothed in left over uniforms from the Civil War, and did not receive changes of uniforms for months at a time.

The end of the War signaled a prideful moment for Negroes, since the black battalions which were allowed to fight in the war performed well and were hailed for their bravery and achievement. This prideful moment made white southerners uncomfortable. They felt that Negroes would take their military training and come back to the South demanding equal rights. Consequently, southern whites started to initiate riots all over the region, killing and lynching Negro soldiers, leaving many of them in their uniforms as they hung from the trees, always making the Negro know in no uncertain terms where their *place* was in the South.

After World War I, the *"Great Negro Migration"* was under way. Many young blacks were emigrating from the rural south looking for employment in the northern cities, especially New York City. As a result, these cities were hopping with the artistic diversity of the highly talented Negro population. This period was coined the *Harlem Renaissance* for the flood of artistic Negroes who made their way to the Harlem neighborhood of New York City. The period only ended with the onset of the Great Depression. During the height of the Renaissance, doors were open to Negroes which had never been open before. Negro playwrights were able to produce, direct, and act in their own plays; Negro authors were able to publish with major publishing houses, and Negro singers and dancers were able to perform at clubs where they were not even allowed to patronize. The interest in Negro culture was extremely high even for white socialites, like Charlotte Osgood Mason, a New York Aristocrat. Her patronage validated the Negro culture for other uptown New Yorkers. This explosion of art demonstrated the Negroes' humanity and promoted their argument for equality.

The Great Depression led quickly into World War II and the Negro population was affected greatly by both catastrophic events. For blacks, finding employment during good economic times was extremely difficult, so getting a job during a depression was nearly impossible. The black unemployment rate was above 50% which was almost 2 times the white unemployment rate. When black people did find jobs they were paid 30% less than their white counterparts. At this rate of pay even if a black person was working, they would still be under the poverty line. President Roosevelt, upon his election, promised to make things better and do it without discrimination. He passed his revitalization legislation called the New Deal, which had nondiscrimination provisions in the bill. However, very few blacks were hired for the New Deal programs and when they were hired; blacks would receive their standard 30% less than whites.

In many ways although life was difficult, Negroes had gotten used to living in dreadful conditions, with very little money coming into the household, so the Great Depression did not cripple them greatly. However, with very few outlets and limited opportunities, many young blacks focused their attentions on furthering their education. Numerous new southern black colleges were producing scores of great students, but few employment options existed in the predominately agrarian south, so the movement of young promising Negroes to the urban industrial north continued at a blistering pace. By the 1940's, this emigration from the south mirrored the first migration, and some sociologist considered this follow up movement of Negroes to be the *"Second Great Migration"*. Millions of Negroes had again left the rural south in order to find their destinies in the big cities of the north. The Negroes still had to face some Jim Crow laws anywhere in the country they went. For instance, on picket lines, some black factory workers were not allowed to picket on the same side of the factory as the white workers. They were required to use separate entrances and even segregated bathrooms within the building, so Negroes could never get completely away from the South. This constant bombardment of negative personal attacks either strengthened Negroes or made them crumble under the pressure; nevertheless those who wanted to find their *American Dream* had to overcome these persistent obstacles which were erected in their path.

The First Lady, Eleanor Roosevelt, took a personal interest in the difficulties of black people. She fought for anti-discrimination policies in the New Deal program so that Negroes could get a fair opportunity at some of the jobs created by the program. Eleanor fought for the passage of the Costigan-Wagner Bill which would have made lynching a federal crime. This bill unfortunately did not pass the Senate because President Roosevelt would not publically support the bill. He did not want to lose the southern democrats who were supporting his progressive agenda. Southern whites hated Mrs. Roosevelt for her outspoken attitude towards civil rights for Negroes. They even blamed her for the Detroit Race Riots of 1943. She, for all intents and purposes, was the Roosevelt administration's liaison to the black community. Even though the administration initiated very few tangible bills to advance the civil rights of blacks, because of Eleanor the Negro vote was now solidly democratic.

The start of World War II witnessed many blacks volunteering or receiving draft notices requiring them to fight for their country. Many Negro soldiers were proud to defend their nation, but quickly started to realize that the Army offered a life style that was no different than the terrible conditions they had to face as civilians. The Army was completely segregated, in some cases worse than the civilian population. The conditions were summed up in a letter from Corp. Rupert Timmingham to the Yank Magazine:

> Here is a question that each Negro soldier is asking," he began. "What is the Negro soldier fighting for? On whose team are we playing?" He recounted the difficulties he and eight other black soldiers had while traveling through the South -- "where Old Jim Crow rules" -- for a new assignment. "We could not purchase a cup of coffee," Timmingham noted. Finally the lunchroom manager at a Texas railroad depot said the black GIs could go on around back to the kitchen for a sandwich and coffee. As they did, "about two dozen German prisoners of war, with two American guards, came to the station. They entered the lunchroom, sat at the tables, had their meals served, talked, smoked, in fact had quite a swell time. I stood on the outside looking on, and I could not help but ask myself why are they treated better than we are? Why are we pushed around like cattle? If we are fighting for the same thing, if we are to die for our country, then why does the Government allow such things to go on? Some of the boys are saying that you will not print this letter. I'm saying that you will."

The Negro soldiers had their own mess hall, latrine, barracks, and units. The black battalions were mostly welcomed when they showed up to report for battle and primarily performed extremely well, gaining commendations from the commanding officers in the field. Few battalions which have been made famous through movies and books were rewarded with the Metal of Honor and many Distinguish Service Crosses. There were other battalions which did not perform so well; most of the time it was because they had an inexperienced commanding officer, so they were badly trained and ill prepared for combat. These battalions also suffered from very low morale resulting from the Jim Crow conditions. But as the War continued and the triumphs of the black battle units became publicized, the attitudes of the other soldiers and military commanders began to change towards an integrated army. Surprisingly, the civil rights movement truly started with great momentum in the armed forces.

With the end of WWII and the reelection of President Harry S. Truman, the country was poised for the wave of civil rights which was ready to sweep through the military. The first shot in the movement was on July 26, 1948, when President Truman issued Executive Order 9981, which effectively abolished discrimination in the armed forces. It also established a mechanism through which the commanders could systematically end all segregation in the military over the next few years. As a result, all segregated units were eliminated by September 1954.

The civil rights movement was now in full force and the Negro community was no longer sitting idly by and allowing Jim Crow laws to continue unchallenged. The 1950's witnessed a flood of court challenges to all aspects of segregation. The NAACP, led by their chief counsel Attorney Thurgood Marshall, was a catalyst in the fight for equality. Attorney Marshall's legal strategy was to challenge these *Jim Crow* laws using the 14th amendment to strike down the *"separate but equal"* doctrine. Plainly, this meant that under the 14th amendment all states must treat its citizens equally and as such, a black person and a white person must be provided equal conditions by the government, and if this is not possible the situation must be integrated, so that each faces the same conditions. In the original segregation argument, southern states stipulated that it is legal to have segregation if they provide equal facilities to both their black and white citizens. However, Marshall illustrated that it was impossible to adhere to the 14th amendment with *"separate but equal"* treatment or facilities. Without giving both a black person and a white person the same treatment or facility, it is impossible for them to be treated equally; one will always have better treatment over the other. Attorney Marshall provided his arguments in *Brown v Board of Education,* and on May 17, 1954 the Supreme Court of the United States returned a 9-0 decision indicating that it is impossible to have a *"separate but equal"* situation, striking down the previous Supreme Court decision from 1896. This new decision opened the door to finally destroying the foundation which permitted Jim Crow laws.

A major victory in the civil rights movement had been attained; it was now just a matter of time before Negroes would be able to overcome the other legal barriers that had impeded their path to equality. The next 15 years were packed with numerous battles over legal access to voting registration without poll taxes and literacy tests and equal treatment in employment and housing. Some of these victories were achieved in 1964 with the passage of the 24th amendment which outlawed the use of poll taxes, and the Voting Rights Act of 1965 which eliminated any further barriers such as literacy test, and further giving the federal government power to oversee all election laws. The Civil Rights Act of 1964 eliminated employer's ability to discriminate based on race, color, sex or national origin, which has been expanded to include sexual orientation and age. The Fair Housing Act of 1968 finally made it illegal to discriminate in renting, selling and financing of housing. Over the following decades these civil and voting rights laws have been amended to better represent our continued fight against discrimination.

The civil and voting rights acts were part of President John F. Kennedy's New Frontier agenda; unfortunately, he was unable to steward his legislative program through the Congress. After President Kennedy's assassination, President Lyndon Johnson, who was a southern democrat from Texas, decided that his best course of action was to see President Kennedy's agenda become law. Accordingly, the 1964 elections resulted in a landslide victory for the democrats which meant that they now had their strongest majority in the Congress since 1938. President Johnson, a congressional veteran, who had held every elected office in the federal government, championed his new <u>Great Society</u> plan which incorporated programs for the elimination of poverty, civil rights for Negroes, and tax reform for corporations and individuals. Of the 252 major legislative proposals, President Johnson was able to get 226 bills passed in the Congress.

The <u>Great Society</u> programs were the largest package of domestic social reforms since the New Deal was enacted after the Great Depression. Along with the civil and voting rights acts, he made the food stamps program permanent, established Head Start, set up the National Endowment for Humanities and the Arts, signed gun control into law, committed federal funding for education, created Medicare and Medicaid, initiated community action programs, and began dozens of youth volunteer programs, most modeled after the Peace Corps. In a speech given by President Johnson at University of Michigan, he summed up his vision this way:

> "The Great Society rests on abundance and liberty for all. It demands an end to poverty and racial injustice, to which we are totally committed in our time. But that is just the beginning.
>
> The Great Society is a place where every child can find knowledge to enrich his mind and to enlarge his talents. It is a place where leisure is a welcome chance to build and reflect, not a feared cause of boredom and restlessness. It is a place where the city of man serves not only the needs of the body and the demands of commerce but the desire for beauty and the hunger for community. It is a place where man can renew contact with nature. It is a place which honors creation for its own sake and for what is adds to the understanding of the race. It is a place where men are more concerned with the quality of their goals than the quantity of their goods.
>
> But most of all, the Great Society is not a safe harbor, a resting place, a final objective, a finished work. It is a challenge constantly renewed, beckoning us toward a

destiny where the meaning of our lives matches the marvelous products of our labor"

Criticism for his <u>Great Society</u> program came from all sides. The conservatives, like Milton Friedman, a Nobel economist from the University of Chicago, School of Economics, understood the political reasons for governments wanting to eliminate poverty; however, he was a staunch advocate of allowing economic growth to provide the means of lifting people out of poverty. He considered the government's fiscal approach to be interference in the markets, thus causing inefficiencies which stop the natural process of markets to adjust and find equilibrium. Government fiscal policy according to Friedman should be focused on tax policy which is outside the market mechanism which will result in the desired acceleration of economic growth. Friedman argued that any artificial priming of the economy should come from the Federal Reserve by way of incremental adjustment to the money supply; not by big fiscal adjustments, allowing the markets to make those larger systematic changes over time.

Friedman and congressional conservatives considered these programs as the further development of the *welfare state*. Johnson's conservative opponents in the Congress and the growing field of republican candidates for president used this idea of a welfare state in order to falsely claim that the typical recipient of the federal dollars was a black single mother who was living leisurely off the taxpayer. This advertising campaign infuriated whites and turned them against the program. White voters began to believe that all their tax dollars were doing was supporting black mothers and their babies, and actually encouraging these black mothers to have more babies so they could get more money. This inaccurate portrayal of the welfare system became the ongoing campaign of republicans, resulting in them winning the public opinion battle with regards to poverty legislation.

Ironically, criticism also came from Dr. Martin Luther King, the most iconic figure of the civil rights movement. Dr. King struggled with the fact that these programs were not coordinated and well thought out. He believed that by starting the vast variety of Great Society programs in such a short period of time, and especially with the backdrop of the Vietnam War escalating simultaneously, these programs could not be thoroughly conceived and would not receive adequate funding because the Vietnam War would siphon dollars which should be used to properly support the war on poverty. As a result, both wars would be inadequately fought because of America's lack of focus. Dr. King was fundamentally against the Vietnam War; being a pacifist, he believed going to war particularly for the purpose of halting the spread of communism was completely wrong, both for the country and in the eyes of God.

Dr. King was precisely correct in his assessment of shortcomings of the President Johnson's Great Society program. As the Vietnam War escalated, all attention and funds were transferred to fighting the war. The financial burdens of the war caused the Great Society programs to struggle from underfunding and also doom the Johnson administration. With public opinion against both the Vietnam War and President Johnson, Republican candidate Richard Nixon used the racist attitudes in the south to finally win a resounding victory and become the President of the United States. However, as history records, even with the financial limitation of the program rollouts, poverty rates fell from 17.3% in 1958 to its lowest level of 11.1% in 1973. Furthermore, the next three presidential administrations of Nixon, Ford, and Carter actually expanded the Great Society initiatives.

The election of President Ronald Reagan in 1980 marked a new beginning in America. President Reagan advocated a new conservative agenda focused on individualism; he advocated "what is good for the individual is good for the nation." Therefore, he wanted to end the welfare state, and create a country based on the Milton Friedman vision of a small government with tax policy focused on massive tax incentives given to individuals and businesses rather than consumers, which he called Supply-side economics. In addition, Reagan initiated outrageous increases in defense spending meant to fill the pockets of his big donors. He justified these defense expenditures by escalating the tension with the Soviet Union through tough tone propaganda speeches. President Reagan articulated this stance in his first *Evil Empire* speech in 1982:

> So, I urge you to speak out against those who would place the
> United States in a position of military and moral inferiority.
> You know, I've always believed that old Screwtape reserved

his best efforts for those of you in the church. So, in your
discussions of the nuclear freeze proposals, I urge you to
beware the temptation of pride -- the temptation of blithely
declaring yourselves above it all and label both sides equally
at fault, to ignore the facts of history and the aggressive
impulses of an evil empire, to simply call the arms race a
giant misunderstanding and thereby remove yourself from the
struggle between right and wrong and good and evil.
I ask you to resist the attempts of those who would have you
withhold your support for our efforts, this administration's
efforts, to keep America strong and free, while we negotiate
real and verifiable reductions in the world's nuclear arsenals
and one day, with God's help, their total elimination

As for his civil rights position, President Reagan on the
basis of states' rights opposed all the civil rights acts and the
voting rights acts. He believed businesses and states should have
the right to serve who they wanted and states should be able to
determine if they want to be segregated. Fortunately, President
Reagan was neither supported by the democratically controlled
Congress nor by many politicians in his own party. Other than
getting his massive tax cuts through Congress, he was unable to
pass any of his social positions through the democratic Congress.
When he did try to veto the Civil Rights Restoration Act of 1988,
the Congress by a two thirds majority in both houses overturned
his veto. President Reagan did sign the Dr. Martin Luther King,
Jr. holiday into law, after realizing the Congress was prepared to
overturn his veto. President Reagan used these positions against
civil rights to maintain his southern political control which
propelled him to his second term victory in 1984.

The 80's witnessed a large influx of immigrants from all
over the world, both legal and illegal. The Hispanic populations
from Mexico and other Latin American countries were growing at

an exponential rate. Also, Asian countries started to flood the United States with immigrants looking for a better life. Most Asians were running away from the tyrannical control of totalitarian governments. President Reagan recognized this immigrant problem, especially with the large number of illegal undocumented workers, so he and Congress in 1986 passed the Immigrant Reform and Control Act. This act required employers to know the residential status of their employees; made it illegal to knowingly hire illegal immigrants; legalized farm workers by giving them temporary work visas; and finally, it legalized all illegal immigrants that came into the country prior to 1982, as long as they paid a fine and any back taxes owed and admitted guilt. This act affected about 3 million illegal immigrants. With respect to black Americans, who had fought so long for equal rights, this act signified the moment when the Hispanic population would inevitably become the largest minority group in America. Between the two groups, it would be only a matter of time before the white population would become smaller than the minority populations. The demographics of America were changing, so must the culture of discrimination.

The new decade saw the election of Vice President George H. W. Bush who was a career politician and public servant. President Bush was first elected to the House of Representatives in 1966 and voted for the Civil Rights Act of 1968. His voting record as a representative was relatively conservative. The eight years he spent as President Reagan's vice president effectively changed his already conservative stance with respect to civil rights making him an even stauncher opponent of the movement. He successfully vetoed the Civil Rights Act of 1990, which tried to stop job hiring discrimination, on the false basis that the act would require employers to have minority hiring quotas. President Bush did sign into law a much less comprehensive bill called the Civil Rights Act of 1991 which provided remedies for racial harassment on the job, but did not address the consequences of discriminatory hiring practices.

President Bush's failure to keep his word on no new taxes doomed his reelection bid in 1992, and opened the door to a presidential candidate many considered to be political long shot. Democratic Governor William Jefferson Clinton, from Arkansas, was a relative political newcomer to the national scene. His high profile introduction to the country came in 1988 at the Democratic National Convention where he gave the keynote address. Governor Clinton was a new generation southern democrat who depended on the support of the African American community for his political success. As a result, Candidate Clinton appealed to the national African American community in order to support his campaign for the presidency. The Clinton campaign machine worked tirelessly to register and foster the African American vote. Governor Clinton represented the first presidential candidate who needed the African American vote in order to be elected. He was not just trying to use the African American vote in order to punish white voters as during the Reconstruction period. In response,

African American voters came out in record numbers in order to support President Clinton. Many have joked that President Clinton was truly the first African American President, which truly could be argued because, as a child in Hope, Arkansas, President Clinton was present on the front lines of segregation and oppression, and although not part of the circumstances faced by African American, he witnessed firsthand the battles for equality.

In reparation to the African American voters who had just put President Clinton into office, he arduously began to fight for black causes such as Affirmative Action. Ever since the mention of quotas, the republicans characterized any program which tried to stop hiring discrimination as a minority quota system. This line of argument greatly enraged the white working class, because they believed the government was making employers hire unqualified black candidates over more qualified white applicants. Of course, this was not the case; Affirmative Action merely tries to level the playing field between white applicants and black applicants. It accepts the premise that white candidates have an inherent advantage over black candidates, in which the advantage could be as simple as the person doing the hiring is usually white, so they probably will have a predisposition to hiring someone who is similar to themselves, which would be the white candidate. By accepting this premise, Affirmative Action just says that employers must at least give the black candidate an opportunity to apply for the position, and if given that opportunity, statistically a certain amount should be hired. The portrayal of Affirmative

Action as a quota system is completely inaccurate. In 1995, with his presidency coming off a resounding midterm election defeat due to his failure with health reform, President Clinton, against the advice of his staff, championed the Affirmative Action Bill and got it through Congress.

With his re-election looming, President Clinton's advisor Richard Morris urged the President to negotiate with House Speaker Newt Gingrich and pass comprehensive welfare reform. Using polling data, Morris showed President Clinton that in order to garnish the white vote in the upcoming election an attack on the welfare state would be his best avenue. Consequently, the Personal Responsibility and Work Opportunity Reconciliation Act of 1996 was the result of their compromise. The act limited the ability of recipients to stay on the welfare rolls for more than two years without searching for work or participating in job training. No claimants could receive more than 5 years of cumulative assistance. This bill rectified the white belief that their tax dollars were being used to support the black single mothers who were just living off the government and having babies.

If we fast forward and look at the effects of the 1996 Welfare Reform Act on poverty, by 2010 poverty rates that had dipped to 11.1% in 1973 were now 15.1%, and children in poverty which was declining before the act has ballooned to 16.4 million, or 22%, by 2010. Instead of focusing on creating opportunities to help people get out of poverty, President Clinton and the Republican Congress pushed more people off the plank without any safety net to cushion their fall. With this one bill, President Clinton allowed the *Age of Individualism* started under Reagan to flourish into the 21st century. Specifically, he allowed the false idea that being poor was solely the responsibility of the impoverished, to continue to dominate our political conversation.

Additionally, the Clinton years witnessed the explosion of the internet; the world was now all connected. Every individual gained a connection to every other person in the world. No one was any longer bound by their surroundings; the internet gave everyone access to an incredibly vast array of information. For the civil rights movement, the internet meant its struggle could go global, and other oppressed people all over the world could join together and rise up against tyranny. We have been onlookers to this incredible phenomenon throughout the last few years with emergence of the *Arab Spring*, where long standing dictatorships all over the Middle East saw an end to their tyrannical reigns. Soon nowhere in the world will totalitarianism be allowed to survive unchallenged. The internet enhanced the importance of individual identity.

After the republicans did everything they could to put Clinton back into his "*place*", even trying to impeach him, Vice President Al Gore chose to run away from the Clinton legacy and run on his own merit. The problem with this strategy was that Gore could not foster the black or Hispanic vote in the numbers which responded to the Clinton appeal. Therefore, Vice President Gore, who should have been a sure thing, lost in a controversial election to Governor George W. Bush of Texas. President Bush ran on a platform of *Compassionate Conservatism*, and being from Texas was very affable to the Hispanic vote. President Bush even spoke fluent Spanish. He was able to garnish a large portion of the Hispanic vote.

The Bush presidency represented merely an extension of the Reagan years. As Reagan did, Bush promoted the *Age of Individualism* with new massive tax cuts meant to spur economic growth, and with the terrorist attacks on September 11, 2001, Bush engaged in two unwinnable wars, which allowed him to similarly fill the pockets of his biggest campaign donors. Bush's war economy and *cowboy* mentality left no room for any other domestic policy objectives. The only social policy objective which President Bush was able to pass was *No Child Left Behind*. This education program attempted to concretely measure how children were performing in schools, and through this flood of data, school systems could determine what, where and why American students were falling behind the rest of the world. However, like Dr. King said decades earlier, programs such as these ill conceived in war time would go completely underfunded, and thusly, although well intentioned, would fail to achieve their high purposed objective. With respect to *No Child Left Behind*, the program has led to additional segregation and isolation of minority students in under performing schools, which because of underfunding were unable to get the resources necessary to improve their situation.

Through the internet, television and other media outlets, these Bush eight years saw a substantial increase in the visibility of black people, especially African Americans. The influxes of immigrants over the last two decades have seen an incredible growth in the number of people with black skin who are not African Americans; blacks who do not have slave heritage. The migration to America has brought people from all the islands in the Caribbean, people from the continent of Africa, and dark skinned people from South America. With Hispanics and Arabs now the minority groups on the radar screens of most white groups, African Americans and other blacks have been able to make strides towards full equality without oppressive whites realizing and trying to put them back in their *place*.

As repressive whites struggled to stop Mexicans from crossing the border and while they were not focused on keeping the *status quo*, blacks edged closer to equality with the election of Barack Hussein Obama as President of the United States of America. Now how are they going to put blacks back in their *place*? Although President Obama is not truly an African American, as his father was directly from Kenya, he surely is the first black American to become president. President Obama in his 2008 election did not go out of his way to court the black vote, but as a former community organizer he was able to motivate at a grassroots level and build upon the inroads made by President Clinton. In retrospect, President Clinton actually did more to entice the black vote to come to the polls, but most black voters wanted to be a part of history, merely seeing President Obama stand in front of the nation and take the oath of office in so few generations removed from *white's only* signs was remarkable all by itself.

The Obama presidency demonstrates that there is so much more which needs to be accomplished in order to reach true equality. Dr. King would have emphasized to all of us that the *journey to the Promised Land* is far from complete. We must stand shoulder to shoulder and keep moving forward. President Obama has faced political opposition which has simply just wanted to see him fail regardless of the impact on the country. Never has a president encountered a Congress which has hated him so passionately that they would totally disregard their love of country. Congressmen have, without any illusions, followed an orchestrated program aimed at making this president a failure, so they can point to his presidency when the next black candidate comes before the American people. It is for this reason why they were so shocked when the community organizer beat them again. *He just doesn't know his place.*

What are the consequences of black history?

Legal recognition of equality was always merely one part of the civil rights struggle for blacks; the other, much more difficult part was the *cultural* acknowledgement of equality. More specifically, white people have to truly believe that blacks are their equals. The contrary must also be true; black people must see themselves as equal to white people. This is especially important for African Americans. The years and years of being portrayed and type-caste as second class citizens, along with the abuse at the hands of white Americans when African American have tried to advance their cause, have taken their toll on the African American psyche. Early leaders of the civil rights movement recognized this sociological identity problem and not only pushed to get the legal barriers eliminated they attempted to strengthen the personal and group identity of African Americans. As a result, African American leaders have attempted to lead African Americans to either believe that they must stand up and be their own nation or they must demand their own place in the American melting pot.

Many leaders have advocated some form of either solution. Early in our history, both whites and blacks were pushing the separate nation answer, each for their own purposes. The modern leaders of the movement learned from the past that there was no going back; there was only moving forward and carving out their own unique path. However, as with most problems, many factions resulted in very different solutions. It was only through the emergence of one leader did black Americans get on the path to the *Promised Land.*

The Republic of Liberia was the initial attempt at creating a nation of ex-slaves established in 1820. It became the consensus in the years prior that repatriation of black slaves to Africa would provide them a better opportunity for equality as opposed to emancipation in America. As a result, Robert Finley, a Princeton University graduate and professor, founded the American Colonization Society in 1816 which began voyages to return freed slaves back to a colony in Africa. This colony was located in the British-ruled Sierra Leone. Primary early funding for this operation came from Paul Cuffee, a wealthy mixed race ship owner from New England, who captained the initial voyages.

Paul Cuffee, a Quaker from Massachusetts, was a devoted Christian who believed in racial equality. Mr. Cuffee was a son of an African slave brought over from Ghana. The Quaker family which brought his father to America freed him when they could not reconcile their Quaker beliefs with slavery. He was in the Ashanti ethnic group, and built a highly lucrative shipping company which gave him the means to open a racially integrated school in Westport, Ma. Mr. Cuffee funded and captained the first few voyages to the coast of Africa. These voyages went to the area known as Sierra Leone where Cuffee, working with the British, established the colony of Liberia. Mr. Cuffee continued his philanthropic work until his death in 1817, at which time the American Colonization Society (ACS) took over the voyages to Liberia, bringing thousands of freed blacks back to Africa over the next thirty years.

The ACS was supported by contributions from many great American figures, such as Henry Clay, John Randolph, and President James Monroe. Although these men were abolitionists, their motivation for supporting the repatriation of freed slaves was far from noble. They were intense racists who did not see any way for emancipated slaves to assimilate into American society. Each felt that ex-slaves with their limited intellect and savage ways would be very troublesome in large number if allowed to stay in America. Moreover, they would take jobs from white workers resulting in a disruptive and unstable country.

On July 26, 1847, the inhabitants of the colony issued a Declaration of Independence, and established a governmental system which was based on the United States constitution. The ACS aided in the development of a constitution, and by 1864 President Lincoln officially recognized the existence of the Republic of Liberia. The country was governed by a party which called itself the True Whig Party. This new ruling group, which consisted primarily of ex-slaves, called themselves Americo-Liberians. They held the reins of power within their small group and kept the other native tribes ostracized, denying them citizenship until 1904. Economically, the country had great difficulty finding markets for their goods and services. In order to pay their ongoing bills they required constant aid from the United States. The government attempted to appropriate international loans, but, became burdened by the debt payments when they were unable to meet the obligations, requiring American aid to relieve the debt situation.

Liberian history from that period forward was marred with great turbulence. The True Whig Party continued to rule the country, inviting corporations from around the world to come and take advantage of the country's resources and cheap labor. The revenues from this economic expansion were being kept in the hands of the Americo-Liberian group, preventing other native citizens from participating in the expansion. This came to a violent end in 1980 when a coup led by the military leader Samuel Doe took over the country, and when the leaders of the oppositional forces tortured and killed the members of the True Whigs government. This coup was followed by the country's first of two civil wars. In the first civil war which started in 1990, saw another faction led by Charles Taylor overthrew the Doe government, triggering a deadly civil war which resulted in the death of 250,000 Liberians and millions of displaced refugees.

A peace deal was signed in 1995 in which Taylor assumed the mantle of President. But by 1999, another faction out of a province located in the northwest corner of the country, feeling alienated by this government, initiated an attack on the Taylor government. This faction was not being represented in government, and therefore demanded participation in the revenues which were coming from the outside corporations. This coup was the first battle of the second civil war, which attracted other factions from all over the country wishing to engage the Taylor government. Finally, in 2005, Taylor stepped down and went into exile in Nigeria. The country was then able to have their first legal and fair democratic election. In 2011, the country had by all accounts another fair and legal election, giving everyone the hope that despite its eventful past Liberia was on its way towards a stable future.

As witnessed from Liberian history, the experiment of trying to create a nation of solely ex-slaves is impossible. Africa, being a very large and diverse continent consists of many tribal factions whom already possess claims over many of the ancestral lands. Over the last ten decades, all tribal groups have demanded their rights to the lands of their ancestors, leaving no room for ex-slaves to claim their unknown birth rights. The only outcomes of such attempts of re-colonization are the resulting conflicts which create an environment of constant civil wars and government overthrows. The perpetual unrest would hardly be in the best interest of ex-slaves coming out of bondage and oppression. Those ex-slaves are at a bare minimum owed by all Americans, especially many who profited from the labor of these black Americans, the opportunity for a better life. All of America, as a nation, cannot simply abandon its obligation of providing for those who toiled so arduously for its development. Black Americans have as much right to pursue the *American Dream*, maybe more, as any immigrant groups who have come to America's shores.

Others have advocated this separate nation philosophy, like Marcus Garvey, a Jamaican that believed all black people who were taken forcibly from Africa should return to their native land.   Marcus Garvey, the editor of a daily newspaper, gave speeches and wrote editorials in newspapers promoting his belief in black supremacy and nationalism. Unlike the motivations of the group behind the ACS, Garvey believed that blacks would be stronger by maintaining a pureness to their race and not intermixing with whites. He actually became allies with leaders of the Ku Klux Klan, who were alternatively promoting white purity. After being deported from the United States, Marcus Garvey continued to articulate his position of Pan-Africanism and push for black superiority. Although his argument was misguided and based on bad assumptions, Garvey was one of the first to recognize the need for group identity building among black people. He realized that only through positive reinforcement of strengths could he uplift the entire race and put them in a position of embracing power as opposed to the powerless posture, which resulted from the degradation they faced everyday from white people. Dr. King at a rally in Kingston in 1965 said, "*Marcus Garvey was the first man of color in the history of the United States to lead and develop a mass movement. He was the first man, on a mass scale, and level, to give millions of Negroes a sense of dignity and destiny, and make the Negro feel that he was somebody."*

As Marcus Garvey did before him, Elijah Muhammad also advocated the establishment of a black nation, through positive reinforcement of black identity. However, he never advocated a *Back to Africa* notion; he believed white people belonged in Europe and only took this nation by force, so black people have every right to establish their sovereign nation here. Additionally, he recognized from Liberian history that blacks who go back to Africa would just be taking land from black brothers who already claim those lands. He believed the destiny of the black man lies right here in America. After the disappearance of his teacher, Elijah Muhammad took over Temple of Islam No. 1 in Detroit in 1935, which gave him leadership and control of the Nation of Islam until his death in 1975.

Mr. Muhammad, who was born Elijah Robert Poole on October 7, 1897, had a fourth grade education, because his parents needed him to work as a sharecropper in order to support their family of thirteen children. By the age of sixteen, Elijah Poole left home and started taking odd jobs in factories and on farms. In 1917, he married Clara Evans from Macon, Georgia. As soon as they could Elijah and Clara became part of the first Great Migration to the north. In the early 20's, they followed thousands of young blacks in pursuit of opportunities in the northern cities which simply were not available in the south. The Pooles eventually settled in Hamtramck, Michigan, a suburb of Detroit.

72

As a black man in the early 30's, Elijah Poole found it very difficult to find and keep a job. Though the Great Depression was horrible for the entire country, it was even worse for young Negroes. Elijah, not being able to provide for his now ever expanding family, and suffering from low spirits, his wife, Clara, encouraged him to attend a speech being given by Wallace D. Fard on Islam and black empowerment.

Wallace D. Fard, who went by many aliases over his lifetime, became later known Wallace Fard Muhammad and founded the Nation of Islam in 1930. In 1933, Wallace Fard Muhammad because of his apparent connection to a ritual murder was told to leave Detroit by the authorities and never to return. W.F. Muhammad left swiftly, but secretly returned to lead the Nation of Islam and propagate his message. However, in June of 1934 Wallace Fard disappeared for good and was never seen or heard from again. Before he left, Elijah Muhammad tells the story of how Fard bestowed upon him the control of the Nation of Islam.

Elijah Poole was one of the first devoted followers of Wallace Fard Muhammad in his Temple of Islam in Detroit. Fard called Christianity the religion of the slave masters, designed to keep black people subservient and under control. The religion promoted race separation and since it was being used by white supremacy groups, such as the Ku Klux Klan, as the foundation for their ideas and values, it must uphold the notions that they claim to be true. He proclaimed Islam to be the original religion of the black man before they became enslaved by their white oppressors. White people covered up this past because they did not want black people to know that they were the chosen group by Allah, the true God, and were the first to inhabit the world. As such, black people were divine by nature, and white people were a race of devils. Elijah Poole found solace and empowerment in these teachings. Wallace Fard Muhammad was able to reach his inner person, and it made everything clear for Elijah. Soon Elijah Poole would discard his slave master given surname, and take on his god given Arabic name of Muhammad.

Although these assertions of Fard Muhammad and later Elijah Muhammad are racist and derogatory towards white people, they were trying to offset two centuries of demeaning and denouncing oppression that black people had to endure. The Nation of Islam was trying to uplift and empower the damaged psyche of the oppressed black man, to give him the power and the resolve to put himself, his family and his God in the forefront of his mind. It provided him the backbone to stand up to those who would put him down, while encouraging him to continue to demand the rights to which he is entitled.

Elijah Muhammad demanded of his followers' upstanding behavior coupled with acknowledgement and ownership for their responsibilities. He expected fathers to foster and be there for their children; he required husbands to respect and care for their wives; he admonished the use of alcohol, tobacco and other narcotics; and most importantly, he preached to black men the need for successful professional lives. These would be based in education and knowledge, and would strengthen understanding of self. Many black men flocked to his temple and as he travelled throughout the country his popularity grew with every new speech or every new gathering. This incredible membership growth, along with Muhammad's unwillingness to interview or meet with any mainstream media organizations, made many, including the government very nervous and suspicious of his activities, labeling his group, *Black Supremacists*.

With fierce rivalries growing in Detroit, Muhammad moved to Chicago and opened Temple of Islam No. 2, where he settled his family until his death on February 25, 1975. Facing constant death threats, Muhammad started moving frequently around the country without his family, opening new temples in major cities. Temple No.3 was opened in Milwaukee, Wisconsin and then he went to Washington, DC where he opened Temple No. 4. However, while in Washington, federal agents arrested him for sedition and failure to register for the draft. Authorities proved the sedition charge by demonstrating that he was encouraging his followers not to register for the draft. As a result, he spent four years in federal prison. While incarcerated, Clara ran the operations of the four temples, and Muhammad continued to preach, read and write, converting many prisoners over to the Nation of Islam. Upon his release in 1946, Muhammad focused his attention on recruiting new leaders for each temple and growing the number of temples and other assets of the Nation. By

1955, there were 15 temples across the country, and then within four years, the number of temples reached 50 in 22 states.

As Muhammad's popularity grew, the knowledge of his movement began to reverberate throughout the black community. Negroes from all over became aware of this movement to empower their people. Friends and family started writing each other to tell them about this organization which was recruiting black men in order to enlighten them about their true religion. Word of mouth was spreading; the word was coursing through the penal system all over the country, and from Muhammad's success with converting prisoners while he was incarcerated, he went out of his way to maintain correspondence with prisoners. For him these men were an ample cradle of recruits.

In late 1948, Muhammad received a letter from a young inmate at the Norfolk Prison Colony, who had been sentenced eight to ten years in prison for robbery. The name of this inmate was Malcolm Little. From Little's letter Muhammad could tell that this was an intelligent albeit troubled young man. He recommended to Malcolm that he should embrace Islam and pray to Allah. Malcolm, who found it very difficult to kneel and pray, forced himself to follow the recommendations of Muhammad. Also, from his early days in prison, Malcolm became an avid reader after he met a very well read inmate named Bimbi who impressed Malcolm with his knowledge of the classics. Bimbi had encouraged Malcolm to borrow books from the prison library and sign up for correspondence classes in order to finish his high school diploma. Knowing Malcolm's propensity to read, Muhammad urged Malcolm to read a list of books in order to educate himself on the teachings of Islam. Malcolm isolated himself and began reading vast amounts of literature on Islamic teachings. Along with reading, Malcolm daily wrote letters to Muhammad and his siblings in order to keep them updated with his new knowledge.

During the remainder of his time in prison, Malcolm perfected his recruitment techniques and through joining the prison debate team, he mastered the art of public speaking. In August of 1952, Malcolm Little was paroled from the Charlestown State Prison. With the help of his siblings, he decided instead of going back to the streets of Boston or New York that he would go and live with his brother in Detroit. His brother, Wilfred, was store manager of a furniture store and he arranged for Malcolm to get a job as a salesman. Wilfred opened his home to Malcolm and taught him the lifestyle of a Muslim. Malcolm started attending services at Temple No. 1, and living the Muslim way of life. He was incredibly impressed with the conduct and manners of the Negroes at the temple. The men were tastefully dressed, and the women dressed in skirts down to their ankles and scarves covering their heads. Even the children were dressed in conservative clothing and very well behaved, respectful to both adult and other children. The entire congregation treated each other with the utmost respect and dignity, using terms like, "Brother", "Sister", "Sir" and "Ma'am".

On the Sunday before Labor Day, Malcolm was finally going to get his opportunity to meet Elijah Muhammad, the *Messenger of Allah*, as he was known to the members of the Nation. A large group of members were driving cars to Chicago to see Muhammad speak in Temple No. 2. Malcolm's excitement was uncontainable. He was looking forward to this meeting more than anything he had ever known. Muhammad greeted Malcolm by pointing him out to the entire congregation. He told the congregation about Malcolm's time in prison, and how he has now devoted himself to Islam and the Nation. Malcolm stood as the members applauded his story. The tribute made Malcolm feel like electricity had raced through his body.

From that moment forward Malcolm Little was no longer. The young brash street thug and ex-con was now reborn as a Nation of Islam leader, Malcolm X. He had discarded his slave shackles and been re-identified by the *Messenger of Allah*. Knowing how hard Malcolm had studied, Muhammad wanted Malcolm to continue his education at an already established temple, so he assigned Malcolm to be the assistant minister at Temple No. 1 in Detroit.

Malcolm X used his skills acquired while in prison and his hustler street smarts to recruit new members to the Detroit temple. He did his recruiting in bars, pool halls, on street corners anywhere he thought he could reach poor naive black people. He wanted to enlighten them and make them aware of how great it was to be black, because they were the truly blessed people, and white people were the devils who were keeping black people down. Soon he was able to increase the membership of the Detroit temple from around two hundred to well over five hundred. It was not easy, but he just kept working tirelessly to bring in members almost one at a time. Elijah Muhammad was so impressed with Malcolm's ability to recruit members that he sent Malcolm to establish the Boston temple, Philadelphia temple and finally to lead the New York temple.

The authorities started to take notice of this new street minister almost immediately. The FBI and the local police worried that this group had become a black supremacy group and was inciting anger and hatred among black people. The FBI came to Malcolm's job in order to ask him why he had not registered for the draft. Malcolm told them he did not think ex-prisoners had to; however, he knew that this was not true. When he went to the draft board, he told them he was a *conscientious objector*. He told the board, "*When white man ask me to go off somewhere and fight and die to preserve the way the white man treated the black man in America, then my conscience made me object.*" The board gave him a deferment.

His next run in with the police left a lasting impression on the authorities. A group of Nation of Islam members were walking by a police arrest of a black man and saw the police beating the suspect. One member, John Hinton, tried to stop the beating, but the Detroit police just arrested him and the other members, also, and when he would not go they started beating

79

Brother Hinton. Malcolm X and a group of Islam members raced to the police precinct where they were holding Brother Hinton. Malcolm insisted on seeing him. A crowd started to grow outside, from just a few hundred to a few thousand in a couple of hours. The police refused to let Malcolm see Brother Hinton who was beaten badly and required medical attention.

With the crowd growing outside, the officers finally agreed to allow Malcolm to see Brother Hinton. Malcolm demanded that Brother Hinton be brought to the hospital so he could receive medical attention. After returning from the hospital, the crowd had grown to over four thousand Negroes. The police allowed the other two Muslims arrested with Brother Hinton to be released on bail, but would not give Brother Hinton bail until after his arraignment the next day. Malcolm, seeing nothing was going to be accomplished that night, walked outside and made a hand gesture and all the Nation of Islam members started walking away, and soon after the entire crowd dispersed. One police officer told the newspaper, "*No one man should have that much power.*" After this incident, Malcolm X was under constant surveillance.

Malcolm X started to gain national and international attention. The Nation's belief in a strong black identity was resonating throughout the black community. Malcolm X became the spokesman and the face of Islam. Mainstream newspapers and magazines wanted to interview this new young dynamic leader and unlike Elijah Muhammad, Malcolm X was not shy about making appearances. He wanted to speak to everyone who would listen. Malcolm X was proud that he was passing on the wisdom of the *Messenger of Allah*, and building the strength of the black race. Conservative observers estimated that the Nation of Islam grew from about 500 members when Malcolm began his membership crusade to more than 40,000 by the early 1960's.

Malcolm X's newfound fame and propensity to crave the spotlight did not impress all members of the Nation. It was apparent that leaders in the Nation were starting to resent his constant media exposure. They believed Malcolm's popularity was overshadowing the true leader of the Nation, Elijah Muhammad. But Malcolm X did not waiver from his methods; he faithfully believed he was spreading the word of the Nation, and the media hovering around his every word was just another way to expand the visibility of the Nation. On the other hand, the media craved the controversial sentiments which flowed from Malcolm's every word. For instance, when asked about President Kennedy's assassination, Malcolm said, "chickens coming home to roost never did make me sad; they've always made me glad." And of the civil rights movement leaders, he called them "stooges" of the white establishment; specifically, he referred to Martin Luther King, Jr. as a "chump".

These and other incendiary statements made him a magnet for the media; however, many in the white community viewed him as a racist, an anti-Semite and a promoter of black hatred towards whites. Malcolm X was one of the most feared and hated

81

leaders in the country. Regardless of what anyone thought of him, he was a devoted follower of Elijah Muhammad and faithful soldier of the Nation of Islam. He not only lived the Muslim life style, he believed its doctrine without any reservations. Consequently, when the rumors started to surface that Elijah Muhammad was having affairs with his secretaries and actually was the father of their children, Malcolm was deeply shaken by the news. At first, he did not want to believe it; these rumors were contrary to everything the *Messenger of Allah* had preached, but as time passed it was obvious that the reports were true. Muhammad confirmed those reports trying to point to other religious prophets which had fallen from grace.

Malcolm X's faith was now shattered. His leader, who he held in reverence just below Allah, was an infidel. In order to regain some level of belief, Malcolm planned a trip to Mecca, the holy city of Islam. This trip changed his life. His international popularity had preceded his arrival; many Muslims had prepared a warm reception for this American Muslim. He was quickly placed in a pilgrimage group going to Mecca. Malcolm immediately started to notice that being Muslim had nothing to do with being black because there were thousands and thousands of white Muslims and Asian Muslims making the same pilgrimage as he was. This was an awakening for him. Being Muslim was about loving and worshiping Allah, and that had nothing to do with one's color. Malcolm was reinvigorated by the kindness of all the different groups of Muslims which he encountered on his pilgrimage.

Malcolm X had travelled like a dignitary, and was welcomed by almost every African leader. He took the opportunity to meet with as many as he could before returning to the United States. This new Malcolm X embraced the civil rights movement, and started to denounce the Nation of Islam, pointing to its limitations as an organization. He realized it could never fulfill its objective as the leader of black people without reaching out to all people regardless of color. He further acknowledged the fact that white people were not devils, only that the racism which was present in America caused them to perform evil acts, and Allah created all races to live together, not merely blacks. Malcolm X met with civil rights leader Martin Luther King, Jr. to discuss their opportunities to work together to further the cause of the black people in America. Malcolm X reached out to white people for support in stopping the *cancer of racism*, which made him in high demand to speak at colleges and universities all across the nation.

These new revelations did not please everyone. Elijah Muhammad viewed this new Malcolm X as a traitor to the Nation of Islam. He told leaders of the Nation that *"hypocrites like Malcolm should have their heads cut off."* Malcolm began to realize that his death was probably inevitable. In somewhat of a foreshadowing his said, *"I know that societies often have killed the people who have helped to change those societies, and if I can die*

having brought any light, having exposed any meaningful truth
that will help destroy the racist cancer that is malignant in the
body of America, then, all of the credit is due to Allah." He
realized that black and white men all across the country were
watching him, merely waiting for the opportunity to kill him. On
February 21, 1965, Malcolm X was shot sixteen times while
giving a speech at the Audubon Ballroom. He was pronounced
died on arrival at the hospital. Malcolm X's death illustrated just
how divided the black community was with respect to achieving
equality. Many openly mourned over the loss of this iconic
figure, while others after investigation were believed to be the
perpetrators of his murder.

Although Dr. Martin Luther King, Jr.'s visit with Malcolm
X was only brief and occurred just once, Malcolm's epiphanies
were consistent with the message Dr. King had advocated since
assuming leadership of the civil rights movement. Dr. King
preached the belief of inclusion and equality for all people,
especially black people. He rejected the notion that either race
was superior; he rejected the idea that black people should have a
separate nation; and most of all, being a follower of Gandhi, he
rejected the contention that anything could be gained through
violence. As Gandhi, he believed in nonviolent resistance,
placing all the burden of stopping the protest on the shoulders of
those who would resort to brutal methods. He believed in the
Christian proverb of "turn the other cheek."

Martin Luther King, Jr. was a Baptist Minister who received his Doctorate in Systematic Theology from Boston University in 1955. Most of his core belief system had its foundation in his strong unflappable adherence to Christian dogma. Through his speeches and later his sermons, he related all his internal principles to his devotion to Jesus Christ and his core philosophy of *Love thy neighbor as you would yourself.* He believed no one who truly loved Christianity could perpetuate the severe brutality that white people use to keep black people *in their place.* Furthermore, he advocated that *one should love thy enemy and pray for them and bless them.* For most this would be an incredibly difficult commandment to follow, especially in the face of all the abuses, lynchings, and beatings that black people had to endure.

From early on in Dr. King's life it was apparent that he had an inherent ability to express himself through public speaking. At the age of 14 one of his beloved teachers took him to an oratorical contest in Dublin, Georgia, which he promptly won giving a speech ironically called, *"Negro and the Constitution."* Also, being the son of a preacher, Dr. King had ample opportunity to refine his craft by watching his father give inspiring sermons. Dr. King's superior abilities did not only involve his ability to orate, he was also academically advanced entering Morehead College at the age of 15 and receiving his Bachelor of Arts degree in sociology by age 19. After leaving Morehead, he was ordained at his father's church Ebenezer Baptist Church in Atlanta and he entered Crozer Theological Seminary in Chester, Pa. to study divinity, receiving his bachelor's in 1951. It was at Crozer where he began his quest to eliminate *social evil*.

His introduction to race relations, like every black person of the south, was immediate and definitive. Atlanta was a completely segregated city; he could not even learn how to swim until a black YMCA was built in the city. When on a city bus, he was expected to go to the back of the bus and even give up his seat to a white person, if the bus was full. In addition, blacks were always expected to sit in the back of the bus, so when no white passengers were on the bus and the back seats were full, black people would be left standing over empty seats merely waiting for a white person to come on the bus. Negroes could not go to just any movie theaters; they had to attend Negro only theaters. This was also true for restaurants and other facilities where blacks and whites had any chance of intermixing. Dr. King despised segregation, and could only dream of the day when he could watch movies and eat anywhere he wished.

Dr. King was able to receive a brief moment of such freedom, when in the summer before attending Morehead he took a job in the tobacco fields in Simsbury, Connecticut. He outlined his eye opening experience in a letter to his father from Simsbury. *After we passed Washington there was no discrimination at all the white people here are very nice. We go to any place we want to and sit any where we want to.* This reality was obviously new to a black man from down south who knew only Jim Crow laws and racial segregation.

Additionally, Dr. King concluded as a teenager that racial injustice resulted in economic injustice. Although because his father was a preacher his family lived quite comfortably, he could see the suffering that his neighbors and friends experienced as a consequence of the segregated south. Jobs for black people were low paying manual labor which did not pay enough for the typical family to stay above the poverty level. Blacks would work arduously and still only have barely enough to feed their families. White people in the same jobs received a better wage and had cleaner working conditions. This fact was never more obvious than when Dr. King in his late teens worked in a plant which hired both white and black workers for a couple of summers. Dr. King could see that the plant owners exploited poor whites and blacks alike, but used each group against the other to demoralize both races. These continued glimpses of social injustice fed Dr. King's burning desire to see societal change.

After receiving his doctorate from Boston University, he accepted his first assignment as minister at Dexter Avenue Baptist Church in Montgomery, Alabama. As he assimilated into the Montgomery social activities, Dr. King joined many groups in different capacities. One of the most prominent groups was the local chapter of the NAACP. Almost immediately after entering the association, Dr. King was informed by the organization's secretary Rosa Parks that he had been elected to the executive committee. About the same time Dr. King started working with the Alabama Council of Human Relations, an interracial group which emphasized that the only way for racial integration to occur was through education of both whites and blacks. Many in the NAACP, who thought integration could only occur through legislation and laws, believed these groups were on opposite sides of the racial issues, and felt that Dr. King's participation in both was a conflict of interest. Dr. King reasoned that both approaches were necessary to see full racial integration. He stated, *"Through education we seek to change attitudes and internal feelings (prejudice, hate, etc.); through legislation and court orders we seek to regulate behavior. Anyone who starts out with the conviction that the road to racial justice is only one lane wide will inevitably create a traffic jam and make the journey infinitely longer."*

Within a year of Dr. King's appointment to Dexter, Rosa Parks, the secretary of the NAACP got arrested for not giving up her seat on the bus to a white person. Although no one predicted it, this incident marked the beginning of the civil rights movement. Contrary to the belief of many, Rosa acted solely of her own accord and at the spur of the moment; she simply had reached the end of her patience, and was not willing to sacrifice her dignity any longer. By the following day E.D. Nixon, president of the Montgomery chapter of the NAACP, contacted Dr. King and they agreed that the further continuation of this act of defiance should be a full Negro bus boycott. Like Rosa, all black people should no longer stand for this type of treatment. They reasoned that blacks may not have legislative or electoral power, but they sure did have economic power. Along with Ralph Abernathy, minister of the Montgomery First Baptist Church, they decided that a bus boycott would be the best course of action.

In amazing speed and organization, the three called together all the black civic and church leaders in order to organize the boycott. All the leaders agreed that the time to talk was over; it was now time to act. The bus situation in Montgomery was a very sore issue with blacks; because they were not only humiliated by being made to sit at the back of the bus, Negroes were insulted and berated by the bus drivers. They were called "niggers", "black apes", and "black cows". Many times Negro passengers had to enter the bus in the front so they could pay, and then get off the bus to go to the back to get on and sit down. Subsequently, it was very easy to get black people to say "*that's enough*". The group set the date as December 5 and made flyers and letters in order to convey the information to all their fellow Negro citizens.

On Monday December 5, Dr. King and his wife, Coretta, woke up earlier than usual to see if the boycott had started. Luckily, there was a bus stop very close to their house. Coretta looked out the window first and started to shout, "Martin, Martin, come quickly!" and as Dr. King ran to the window to his amazement, he shouted, "Darling, it's empty!" There was not a black person on the bus. The South Jackson line which passed by

Dr. King's house carried the most Negro passengers in Montgomery. The city Negro leadership had thought they were going to get approximately 60% participation in the boycott but from all indications over 90% of Negroes were respecting the boycott. Dr. King jumped in his car and drove all over Montgomery looking inside buses, and to his astonishment almost all the buses were empty. The boycott continued all day long; at afternoon peak hours the buses were still empty. Negroes were walking, riding mules, horse drawn buggies; people who had cars were driving other people to work. Whatever needed to be done to get to work, black people were doing it.

With this miraculous show of solidarity, it was agreed upon that the boycott would continue until certain demands were met. However, they had to get consensus from the rest of the Negro citizens, so they called a meeting for that very night. Dr. King was elected to give the speech which would change his life forever. He would become the face of the movement. The question of whether most of the Negro citizens were behind the boycott was immediately made academic. The Holt Street Church was packed to the rafters; it was a standing room only crowd. The black people at this small church were empowered with a burning desire for equality. All Dr. King had to do in his speech was stoke this fire, without making the flame too hot, so that they could maintain their Christian values.

Dr. King's speech was brilliant and moving, grabbing the crowd and inciting them while still holding them within his amazingly strong presence in order to maintain their calm. Everyone in the crowd could feel the power and strength of their movement, and the possibilities of their destiny which was born from their unity. Black people for the first time felt empowered and strong. Negroes finally felt they could carry the weight of their cause and shoulder the burdens of their future. This brief moment in history uplifted an entire race to continue forward and overcome the oppression which had seemed so insurmountable. Dr. King was the voice but the Negro citizens were the body and the soul.

The boycott was in full force. Most Negro citizens were finding different means to get to work and the city leaders of Montgomery were beginning to resort to any methods possible to break the boycott. They even tried to lie by releasing a news report that a group of black ministers had made a deal with the bus company and the boycott was over. Dr. King and the other civic leaders rushed to find out which ministers betrayed the movement. Within hours it was determined that the city leaders had completely fabricated the report. Dr. King immediately got the word out that the report was a lie, and all Negro citizens maintained the boycott. In response, the mayor then initiated a program of "*get tough*" on Negroes. He denounced the boycott and said that it did not matter "*if a Negro ever rode the bus again.*" However, Montgomery police started to arrest Negroes for minor offenses, and Dr. King, now being the face of the movement, was one of the targets of the operation.

The police began following Dr. King as he drove around town. Dr. King had expected that he would be jailed sometime as the movement progressed, he did not imagine it would be so soon. The police finally arrested him for going thirty miles per hour in twenty five miles per hour zone. As the officers drove with Dr. King he noticed that they were not bringing him to the police station. Fear began to grow within the his mind. He could only think that they were bringing him to an awaiting mob ready to kill the leader of the movement before it started. The panic in his mind grew; he could only pray to God that he would have the strength to face the events which were about to come. Then in the distance, Dr. King saw a light, and as they drove closer he could read the words, *Montgomery City Jail*. With an ironic sense of relief, he could exhale and breathe smoothly as he felt an incredible weight lift off his chest. Never before did he think that he would feel so relieved to see he was going to jail.

As Dr. King entered the jail, he noticed that there were cars full of Negroes lining up outside the gates. The crowds were growing; it was at that moment when Dr. King realized that he was not alone in the movement, and the courage which he had lost on the ride in the police car he quickly regained. Now it was affirmed, black people stood together against the tyranny which had oppressed them all their lives. With the crowds growing, the city officials decided the best option was to release this magnetic figure instead of letting him become a lightning rod for the movement.

The Montgomery bus boycott eventually ended with the Negro citizens getting the buses desegregated, both through court order and societal pressure. Dr. King was one of the first to ride the newly desegregated buses. The greater lesson learned was the knowledge that this formerly weak oppressed group of Negro citizens, although still oppressed, really had power; they had strength in numbers. The hope for equality was no longer an unrealizable fantasy; it was an achievable destiny. Dr. King knew that this movement was inevitable and would exist without him; he truly felt blessed to stand on the shoulders of the great Negro people.

This sense of humility drove Dr. King to learn more about the principles of nonviolent protest; consequently, with the help of a Quaker organization he took a trip to India in order to learn the techniques of nonviolent resistance from the writings of Gandhi. From his visit he realized that Gandhi had learned his understanding from Tolstoy who based his knowledge off of the life of Jesus. As a result, Dr. King could see not only was the cause just, his methods of implementation were equally blessed by God. This knowledge reinforced his faith in the movement. Moreover, the word of his crusade had spread internationally. He became a hero to those who wanted to end oppression worldwide, and so Dr. King took this opportunity to rally world leaders in support of his fight for Negro equality.

Before Dr. King's pilgrimage, the movement had expanded outside of Montgomery to all areas of the segregated south. The movement was attracting college students and frustrated black adults from all over the country. Dr. King and the other leaders of the movement formed the Southern Leadership Conference in which Dr. King was named the president. This group later became known as the Southern Christian Leadership Conference (SCLC). The purpose of the organization was to coordinate the actions of local protest groups all over the south, and act as the national focal point for the movement.

Dr. King was at the center of the national spotlight on the civil rights movement. He received death threats from both white and black groups alike. The white groups wanted to put this *nigger* back into his place, and the black groups thought his nonviolent approach was cowering down to their white masters, illustrating that blacks were weak with no backbone. Dr. King's "*brush with death*" came quickly. At a visit to Harlem, in order to do a signing for his book on the Montgomery bus boycott, a black woman approached him and simply asked, "*Are you Martin Luther King?*" Before Dr. King could fully respond the lady, Mrs. Izola Ware Curry, plunged a letter opener into his body. Dr. King was immediately rushed to Harlem hospital where a team of doctors removed the letter opener, and stitched close the wound.

Dr. King had been jailed and almost assassinated and this was just the start of the movement. It was apparent that at some point in the future this movement would have to survive without him. Additionally, it was also evident that *nonviolent resistance*, as it had done for Gandhi, was frustrating those who would like to see the movement fail. While he recovered in the hospital, Dr. King was reaffirmed that he had to prepare the movement to proceed without him, because he probably would not make it *"up to the mountaintop"*, and he would have to inspire all Negroes in the movement to stick to nonviolence regardless of the brutality which would be caste upon them. Only through their adherence to nonviolent protest would they hold *"redeem not only America but the world."*

The years which followed saw great strides for the movement, such as the sit-in at lunch counters in Greensboro, NC and the Birmingham protests, where Dr. King was jailed again, as well as incredible milestones for a man so young in years. Dr. King was humbled by all that the movement had bestowed upon him; he had the opportunity to have audiences with presidents, sit side by side with kings and queens, and most notably he won the Nobel Peace Prize for his leadership in the struggle. Through all these accolades, Dr. King never forgot that he was just a lowly servant of God and the cause of the Negro people. Nothing he had accomplished could he have done without Jesus being his inspiration and the Negro people being the movement's body and soul.

On his flight to Oslo, Norway, Dr. King could not mentally reconcile why he had won this recognition until he realized that this was not solely a tribute to one man's contribution to history. The Peace Prize represented an acknowledgement of what thousands of people in the struggle have done and will do in the years to come. It is not the indication that the struggle is over, it is merely the reaffirmation that the struggle must carry on and he as the leader was simply a conduit for the message that the movement must continue to persevere. Dr. King knew at that moment he was accepting this honor for all upon whose shoulders, he stood.

In his acceptance speech, Dr. King looked forward to where the movement would take the country and the world. He did not fail to commend those who brought the movement this far, but he wanted to emphasize just how long the journey was still going to be. He also highlighted many who could not stand there with him, like Nelson Mandela, who was imprisoned in South Africa, and were not able to experience the changing world. He praised President Johnson for his push for a Great Society, and challenged the world to join the war on poverty. Finally, with the Vietnam conflict starting to brew, Dr. King warned the world of the necessity to accept the convention of nonviolence. He implored world leaders to find alternative ways to solve their conflicts, because wars and battles have merely killed many, but have never completely solved any dispute. With this he ended, *"Racial injustice around the world. Poverty. War. When man solves these three great problems he will have squared his moral progress with his scientific progress. And more importantly, he will have learned the practical art of living in harmony."*

After the speech and the dinner and Oslo were a distant memory, Dr. King reflected on the future of the movement. He found himself having more conviction and a stronger determination than he had ever had before. The Prize had truly stoked the fire which was burning inside of him; he reiterated this newly discovered motivation at a dinner in Atlanta held in recognition of the Prize. He proclaimed that he had to descend off this *mountaintop* and re-enter the *valley* filled with "*agonies, dangers, and frustrating moments."* Because he knew the "*valley filled at the same time with little Negro boys and girls who grow up with ominous clouds of inferiority forming in their little mental skies; a valley filled with millions of people who, because of economic deprivation and social isolation, have lost hope, and see life as a long and desolate corridor with no exit sign. I must return to the valley...."*

Dr. King and the movement were from this point forward inseparable. He had stood tall in Washington, walked forthright and strong through Selma, and boldly sat at the negotiating table in Chicago. Wherever he went newspaper reporters followed his every step; they were captivated by his every word. His almost iconic popularity threatened all those who saw the movement as an attack on their way of life. The notion that killing "*the nigger King*" would only make him a martyr was forgotten, "*the nigger had to die*" was the thought of the day. Death threats followed the movement to the next location; white assassins were lining up to pull the trigger. Dr. King knew that it was merely a matter of time before someone would try and possibly succeed at killing him; he hoped that he had adequately prepared the movement for the journey to come, because he knew the quest would be arduous and long and continue well into the future. So even if he could have had a long life, at some point the movement would have to go on without him. On April 3, 1968 in Memphis, Dr. King left the movement with this message,

> Well, I don't know what will happen now. We've got some difficult days ahead. But it doesn't matter with me now. Because I've been to the mountaintop. And I don't mind. Like anybody, I would like to live a long life. Longevity has its place. But I'm not concerned about that now. I just want to do God's will. And He's allowed me to go up to the mountain. And I've looked over. And I've seen the promised land. I may not get there with you. But I want you to know tonight, that we, as a people, will get to the promised land. So I'm happy, tonight. I'm not worried about anything. I'm not fearing any man. Mine eyes have seen the glory of the coming of the Lord.

The next evening, Dr. King was shot while standing on the balcony of the Lorraine Motel. After he was rushed to the hospital, surgeons tried to save him but he was pronounced dead on the operating table. As Dr, King foreshadowed, he would die as Gandhi did before him; his life would be shortened by those who could not stem the tides of his cause. They may have succeeded in taking his body from this earth that night, but his vision lives on in us all.

Many have tried to carry on the mantle for the movement, but no one has been able to motivate the body while captivating the soul of the Negro people. Dr. King raised the status and the prestige of all black people by showing them the value each person has inside. He started the process towards healing the African American psyche, illustrating through his own personal journey that every black individual was inherently equal to whites, and do have a place in the American melting pot. Many leaders have had good intentions and have tried to offset the years of abuse, but only Dr. King was able build the confidence of the African American without attacking the status of others. He raised African Americans up without bringing anyone else down. Dr. King, as his final message to us all, demonstrated that only through the uplifting of African Americans can equality finally be reached.

Jesse Jackson, a civil rights activist under Dr. King in 1965, has tried to assume the role of leader over the last four decades, but has not been able to unite the factions that fragmented after the death of Dr. King. In addition, immigration has brought to America many blacks that did not have the same southern slave heritage, so getting their full participation into the movement has been difficult. Jesse Jackson recognized these changing demographics and tried to unite all minority groups through his organization the *Rainbow Coalition* which he founded in 1984 prior to his first run for President of the United States. In his second run for president in 1988, he continued his quest to bring all minority groups together, which is when he coined the term *African American* to encompass all black people from all nations. This label, however, did not have much meaning to blacks from other countries because they already considered themselves "*blank*" Americans, whether for example, Jamaican or Kenyan. This label did give black Americans with southern slave heritage a sense of identity. They were now given a uniform cultural ancestry. Beyond this, Jesse Jackson or any other leader could never bring together all the many divisions of African Americans under a single umbrella. As for all minority groups, their agendas and beliefs of how and what needs to be accomplished are way too vast for anyone to unite even for the single purpose of equality.

When must America focus on African Americans?

African Americans and many other blacks realize the struggle continues, despite the election of the first black president. However, America is at a moment in history where the status of minority groups in the United States will change forever. With minority populations rising, these next few decades will be a struggle for the previous generations of white European Americans to maintain their singular dominance. Although legislation will be introduced as if times have not changed, the days of white versus black can never be seen again. With the inflows and growth patterns of all other groups, this conservative grasp on the past will be a distant memory. The bipolar country we have been for the last few centuries will cease to exist and we will be faced with a multi-racial nation. This new nation will have changing problems and concerns, forgetting about the old battles which are not yet finished. These conflicts will be cast aside and those who are still victims of the fallout will be left to deal with their own traumatic injuries. A common pattern throughout its history, America has too many times exited one battlefield merely to enter another without dealing with the wounded warriors' leftover from their previous actions.

The future of America is intricately tied to the successes of each and every group that will call themselves Americans. African Americans have always been a group uniquely devoted to

101

the development of the United States. They have demonstrated their loyalties and patience, even in the face of complete outright rejection. As Dr. King said, "If not now, when…", the time has come. The situation of the African American will only be an afterthought as we transition into a new reality. African Americans have struggled long and hard, holding tightly to the promise which is the bedrock that makes America the greatest nation ever conceived. They have accepted the notion that tomorrow will be a better day, embracing the belief that America will someday hold to its creed. There are many who believe that because of this evolution, America is in a decline; however, those people fail to understand what has truly made America great. It is not the race or origin of those who have come here; it is the belief that when someone arrives they will have a fair opportunity to rise to any height their talents can take them. Without this possibility, America would truly be on the decline. America will only be judged by how it provides opportunities for its people, because that is the sole benchmark which matters. So as America transitions into a new nation, it cannot forget about the group which was forced to come to its shores and made to arduously labor for its growth and success.

African Americans have consistently lagged other immigrant groups in their development and movement into the economic and political *Promised Land*. Responsibility for these results lies squarely at the feet of those who have taken from this group the opportunities for which America has promised all its citizens. It is the obligation of every American to make certain that we no longer obstruct African Americans and allow them to equitably progress forward towards the *American Dream*. African Americans, contrary to many opinions, have never lacked the effort or determination to strive and succeed. As their history illustrates, they have just encountered insurmountable obstacles that have stood as barriers in their way; and still they persevered, reaching a moment in history where full equality is not only attainable, it is within reach. But the last few impediments are the most difficult, because they require a cultural transformation. In order for the future to change, America must completely understand the hurdles which African Americans are required to overcome.

America fails to remember that we are only six or seven generations removed from when African Americans were in shackles, and again this is neither an excuse nor a justification, it is simply a fact. Over that time, as history illustrates, much of America has continued the slave master treatment and definitions of black people. Even with President Lincoln freeing all slaves, the hearts and minds of many white people have not changed with respect to their subservient view of a black person. These attitudes have flooded over to all black people regardless of cultural origin, and as the nation becomes more diverse this belief system is being projected on to all people of color. Consequently, the specific treatment of African Americans has resulted in problems which are deeply rooted in the slave culture of the past.

103

Particularly, many of the social and economic issues which African Americans face today find their essential beginnings in the behavior of slave masters.

The most significant socioeconomic issue plaguing the African American community today is the dissolution of the family unit. The reasons and consequences of this lack of family dynamics have far reaching implications throughout the entire African American community. At its very core, this problem has direct roots in the cotton fields of the nineteenth century. After the Emancipation Proclamation, the erosion of the family was a manifestation of the dismal economic conditions and the segregation which continued through the next one hundred years leading up to the civil rights movement. As years have passed, a further factor is the extremely high incarceration rates of African American males which has removed those males from the family structure and left a void of parental guidance. Finally, the governmental policies developed with the intention of combating the impoverished conditions because they were inadequately thought out actually added to the persistent destruction of the African American family.

The family unit represents the fundamental building blocks of every society. All other immigrant groups have built their assimilation into the American society directly from the cohesion of their family structures. Asian, European, and Latin Americans erected their foundations solidly on the backs of their immediate and extended families. Then, through the diligence of generations after generations of each layer of family members helping all others to succeed, they are able to reach the American dream; every generation pushing the next generation to reach further and further towards their *more perfect union.*

African Americans simply did not have these family members available to support the growth of a well developed family tree. One early reason was that many genealogies would have discovered branches of family trees which had interracial relationships, and those white lineages did not want to be uncovered. Another issue which influenced this incomplete family structure that also persists today was the high number of out of wedlock births. In 2010, births to black single mothers accounted for 72% of all black births, as opposed to only 29% of white births. It is true that births out of wedlock are much more prevalent presently, and this incredibly high number further decreases the likelihood of family attachments. Though statistics are not readily available, because the marriage rates of slaves were very low it is reasonable to infer that births out of wedlock occurred at an extremely high rate resulting in a fragmented family structure. Also, due to methods such as slave breeding, crimes like rape and sexual assault, and just simply family separation ensuing from sales of slaves, slave masters destroyed slave family cohesion.

Although many different views have surfaced concerning slave breeding, it seems only logical, as the country outlawed importing slaves and the cotton crop was booming, slave masters would resort to breeding slaves. Also, since slave masters treated slaves as live stock, producing slaves through controlled reproductive means would create a new slave to sell or put to labor without the added overhead cost of going out and buy another slave at auction. The legislation banning the importing of slaves led to a shortage as the southern economies grew, so inflation in the price of slaves made buying slaves at the auction very pricey. Regardless, when breeding was used slave masters would mate the strongest black males with fertile females in order to yield the most robust offspring. The males would not be allowed to stay with the family units and raise these children; most of the child rearing was be done by the females.

Furthermore, slave masters would frequently rape slaves or merely use them as their sexual objects. The children who resulted from these relationships by law would also be slaves. The masters in most case disassociated themselves from the children and left the raising of these children up to the mothers in these relationships. Also, when black male slaves would have interracial relationships with white southern women, the fathers of these children were either killed for raping the white females or sold; the resulting children were auctioned off or the child and the mother were sent away. The number of mulatto slaves increased by a rate of almost 100% in just ten years. From the 1850 census data workers identified 245,000 mulatto slaves in the country, and by 1860 there were almost 450,000. Slave masters would sell off their illegitimate children as soon as they became of working age.

Frederick Douglass was a famous ex-slave who escaped to the north, and was able to break the law and learn to read and write. In his biography, he described his own experience as an illegitimate child of his master. Mr. Douglass was separated from his mother before the age of 1, and given to an old slave woman to raise and care for. His mother was sold off to a farm about 12 miles away. He only remembered seeing her about four or five times in his life, when she would walk the 12 miles to see him, and those times were short because she had to walk back before dawn.

Black families which had children through normal relationships would try to keep these family units together; however, it was always uncertain how long slave masters allowed families to stay together. If black males were not needed to produce in the fields, they were sold at auction to increase the wealth of the plantation owner, and as stated above this practice was done as young as twelve or fourteen years of age. Black females upon entering puberty were sold into prostitution as concubines or simply to other plantations as slaves. This tenuous situation made many parents encourage their children to attempt to escape the bondages of slavery before the slave masters could sell them as cattle. Either way these family units were ripped apart, leaving each member with a limited number of relatives to depend on. Therefore, not only were immediate families members separated, extended families members could not be found.

After the Civil War and during Reconstruction, the destruction of the black family unit continued. The economic conditions and the institution of segregation, implored black children to leave home as soon as possible in order to allow their families to continue to feed the remainder of their younger siblings. Fathers had to venture away from the family to find work so that they could send money back to care for young children. On black farms, as stated earlier, much of the harvest was paid as rent to large plantation owners for the right to cultivate the land. The children who could not add to the production on the farm would leave the farm in order to relieve the family of the burden.

The Great Migrations illustrated this movement of African Americans away from the agrarian south to the large urban areas of the north. The industrial growth of the north attracted young African Americans seeking an opportunity to achieve the American dream. However, this dream was mostly unsatisfied because African Americans exchanged the explicit racism of the south for the implicit racism of the north. Although the northern states did not practice segregation, African Americans were pushed and steered into black only communities, which later became urban ghettos. African American unemployment in these urban areas consistently averaged 10-20% above the rate of white Americans. In addition, when African Americans did find jobs they received on average 30% less pay for the same jobs. Some recent studies argue that most of this difference can be accounted for by the gap in educational preparedness. During this most recent recession, and for that matter any recession before, the black community is more harshly affected by the cyclical downturn. Normally, the unemployment rate of black males is twice that of white males, however, during the peak of a recession, the unemployment rate for black males spike at two and half to three or four times the rate of white males; black males are the last to be hired and the first to be fired. White employers relegated African Americans to more menial jobs, believing that African Americans were not capable of performing jobs which required higher skill sets.

This consistent portrayal of black workers as inferior to white workers, both in their intellectual capacity and in their capability to do higher level labor activities, persistently affected African Americans' ability to provide for their families, requiring African Americans to find multiple employment opportunities, which were usually very scarce. Many African American had to resort to "*hustling*" and other criminal activities in order to generate money needed to bring their families to a basic subsistence level. These urban areas fostered a hot bed of activities, such as promoting the sale of drugs, pushing the business of prostitution, and encouraging petty theft and robbery. African Americans became the frontline salesmen for the illicit goods demanded by the white population.

In response the judicial system has, without imprudence, punished the black suppliers while allowing the white purchasers of the illegal merchandise to go free and continue satisfying their desires. It is estimated that African Americans make up only 13% of drug users, but they represent 74% of those sent to prison. The imprisonment of black Americans in the United States has reached epidemic proportions. This methodical and systematic use of an inherent judicial bias, moreover, has made the black male an endangered species. Similar to slave masters removing black males by sale at auction, this pervasive utilization of the judicial system to incarcerate black males has left African American families unable maintain a cohesive connection. Black males in 2009 accounted for 40% of all prisoners in both state and federal correction facilities in the United States, whereas black males only made up 6.4% of the overall population. Furthermore, a study by the Bureau of Justice Statistics found that it was significantly more probable, 20 to 57 times, for black males to be imprisoned at younger ages than white males. It is noteworthy that the judicial system is now including Hispanics as a targeted group for imprisonment. The likelihood for a young Hispanics to be incarcerated is increasing dramatically.

The consequences of this attack on young black males have far reaching implications. Not only are black families suffering from the lack of male role models and fathers, black males with felony convictions have an even more difficult time finding gainful employment. Black males' ability to leave a legacy is diminished by their simple inability to acquire life insurance or other assets to pass on to heirs. Most profoundly, black males are unable to participate in the political process which places all African Americans at a disadvantage with respect to influencing the direction of the country. The characterization of drug crimes as felonies with mandatory sentencing has caused many black males to end up in prison and also be disenfranchised. Over 1.4 million black males have permanently lost their right to cast a ballot. The inability of black males to vote allows those who would continue the oppression to have the means in which to pass policies that inhibit the future progression of all African Americans.

Another implication is the urban poverty which resulted from the shortage of black males available to financially support their families. The vicious cycle of lack of jobs in urban areas leading to the necessity of criminal activities in order to support one's family then the incarceration for those crimes, have left families broken and in need as they were before. Mothers and children are left to suffer the consequences for their fatherless homes. In a book by William Julius Wilson, When Work Disappears, he found that *"44% of black women living with their children in Chicago's inner city have no other adults in the households, only 6.5% of Mexican women are the sole adults in their household. Also, inner-city black women whose children are under 12 years of age are eight times more likely than comparable Mexican women to live in a single-adult household."*

Poverty in urban areas was a product of the overflow of blacks from the southern agrarian economy. Although these southern blacks actually performed better than their northern counterparts with respect to finding employment, they created a surplus supply of labor in the urban areas. With work in these cities moving into the suburbs, the poverty rates were escalating. As outlined by Wilson, these black ghettos of the 60's, 70's and 80's resembled the urban ghettos of the 1930's where segregation and isolation created a cauldron of extreme poverty, where 32% of African American families in 1980 were below the poverty level, as opposed to 10% of white families. As of 2009, the percentage of African American families in poverty had started to rise again to 25% after hitting a low in 2000 of 22%. White families in poverty during the same period hit an all time high of 12% in 2009 after reaching a low of 9.5% in 2000.

President Lyndon Johnson attempted to solve this problem of poverty, but as acknowledged by Dr. King, any program begun in a time of war would have to be underfunded and secondary to the needs of the country. Due to lack of forethought and funding, the creation of the welfare state although well intentioned, did not allow for black males to come back into the families and resume their roles as fathers and providers. If black families were to stay together, aid would be shut off even before families could establish the ability to support themselves. But President Johnson was able to reduce poverty from 15% to 11%. In 1996, under a renewed sense of individualism, President Clinton and a republican led Congress, without much thought to the family implications further reformed the welfare program giving recipients two years of benefits with a maximum of five years over one's lifetime regardless of financial condition. This bill also excluded the male from the household placing all the pressure on the female to provide for the family, and requiring the male to do anything necessary to support from the outside. Since the inception of Clinton's welfare reform, the percentage of people in poverty has climbed back to pre-Johnson *War on Poverty* campaign levels of 16%. In an extended slow economy, it is very difficult to find or train for employment in the period which recipients are given, causing mothers and children to slip further into poverty.

An alarming statistic from the National Center for Children in Poverty is that children in poverty as a result of this reform has risen by 21% for 2000 to 2008, meaning there are 2.5 million more children living in poverty in 2008 than 2000. A large percentage of these children are a result of this urban cycle; as of 2008, 35% of black children live in poverty as opposed to 11% of white children. The growing number of children in poverty is having a measurable effect on the educational system. The educational achievement gap between white students and black students has been consistently increasing. This gap even increases over the years if the students start with similar scores only a few years earlier, which indicates that the home life of blacks persists in impeding their advancement. The number of black students who graduated for the school year 2009-2010 was 472,261. These graduates represented 66% of freshman who started four years earlier. In contrast, 1,871,980 white students graduated high school, which was 83% of all freshmen who began. This gap represents a major loss to the black American community.

Although there are many factors associated with the inability to complete a college degree, the difference between the races increases steadily for the college years. For white students 62% of freshmen for academic year 2002 completed their 4 year degrees in at least six years, whereas only 42% of black students completed their degrees. Not to make excuses, the same inherent problems discussed previously such as lack of family support, results in the need to find immediate employment; and children out of wedlock which without childcare provided by relatives makes it impossible to finish school programs. In addition, the inferior schools located in the ghetto areas produces students who are ill-prepared for the demands of a rigorous college curriculum. This loss of intellectual achievement has rippling effects throughout the entire community for generations.

These segregated black urban ghettos caused schools in those areas to suffer from lack of funding, bad teachers, and disruptive students producing a substandard education for all the students who attend. America is seemingly losing an entire generation of African American students to schools which are well below performance levels of schools in white areas. The reasons for these under achieving schools vary, but most are caused by the insufficient representation by elected officials to fight for these schools to receive adequate supplies of anything. The ghetto schools receive the last of everything, even teachers, and are the first to get cut when budgets have to be trimmed. The black populations in these areas, as illustrated earlier, through disenfranchisement do not have either the opportunity or the wherewithal to exercise their voting rights, so they are ignored by politicians. In a study by the American Sociological Association, a black child who grows up in a ghetto is 20% less likely to graduate high school than a black child who lives in an affluent neighborhood, so where one resides matters greatly.

Accordingly, white real estate agents by design and sometimes through buyers' preferences have been directing black home buyers and renters into areas which were predominately black. Thus, though Jim Crow laws did not exist in the north, black and white housing became very segregated creating these urban ghettos and affluent black communities, with few integrated neighborhoods. As determined in Brown vs. Board of Education, any type of "*separate but equal*" is pragmatically impossible. John Yinger in his book, Closed Doors, Opportunities Lost, The Continuing Costs of Housing Discrimination, investigated the roots and repercussions of housing discrimination. Although the Fair Housing Act of 1968 was passed to eliminate the prejudice in housing decisions, Yinger found that blacks, and to a lesser degree Hispanics, still face discrimination on both a systematic and individual level. He reasoned that housing segregation was not completely caused by white prejudice. Many factors attribute to creating segregated neighborhoods, such as buyers preferences to be in neighborhoods of like kind of people. But when many white buyers in Detroit were asked would they move into neighborhoods that were predominately black, 30% of white buyers responded that they were willing to move into neighborhoods that were up to 53% black. However, overall in the case, *Freeman v. Pitts,* the US District Court in its summary to the Supreme Court stated that housing segregation is a product of private preference because the court heard evidence that on average a white buyer prefers neighborhoods which consists of an 80-20 split, whereas black buyers prefer a 50-50 ratio. The court concluded that there were no constitutional implications, merely personal choice.

Regardless of the reasons for segregation, the lack of integration has damning effects for those who live in the politically under represented areas. First, as shown above the school systems in that area become rundown and underperforming due to the deficiency in resources. Secondly, the housing values in those areas decrease responding to the subpar quality of the housing in the neighborhoods, meaning dwellings in these areas are usually significantly older and much less maintained both by the city and by individuals. Thirdly, mortgage discrimination triggers a domino effect which results in more foreclosures and short sales which bring down property values even further. Specifically, lenders are in the business of lending their money and receiving it back with interest, and they have systematically found black buyers and black neighborhoods to be riskier investments. As a result, they have charged black buyers moving into predominately black neighborhoods or elsewhere higher interest rates and higher closing costs, making significantly more money on the front end of loans just in case they do not receive all their principal back. The obvious problem with this practice is that it perpetuates the cycle which they caused in the first place. As a side note, since someone's home is usually their largest tangible asset, this system greatly influences African and Hispanic Americans' capacity to build wealth and prosper.

Fourth, one of the businesses which vacated the urban areas was grocery stores and supermarkets, taking with them the access to fresh fruits, vegetables and other nutritious foods, leaving behind only convenience stores, high fat restaurants, and greasy dives. Additionally, with the residents of the ghettos unable to purchase private health insurance, doctor visits for preventative care and needed medical procedures which would catch ailments before they develop into life threatening diseases, were overlooked or simply ignored. Most medical conditions resulting from an inadequate diet, such as diabetes and cancer, are not diagnosed until they become acute. President Johnson created Medicaid in order to help the extremely poor have access to some of the necessary health services. However, as of 2008, 17% of black people still remained without any health insurance coverage, whereas only 9.9% of white people. The disturbing number is that 30% of Hispanics were without health insurance coverage.

Finally, in a vicious cycle, housing segregation in urban areas has driven out many additional businesses that were unable to survive with only limited income clientele and a less skilled workforce. Accordingly, most of the jobs associated with these businesses followed them into the suburban areas, leaving the urban areas devoid of opportunities. In the Great Recession of 2007, unemployment rates for black males peaked around 22%, whereas white males reached approximately 7%. Many theories have surfaced to explain this inability of blacks to find employment openings out of the urban areas. One such theory relates everything back to housing discrimination; the spatial mismatch hypothesis states that because of housing discrimination black workers are unable to move into the suburbs where the businesses have relocated, so they are restricted from progressing through the natural adaptive process. Yinger additionally writes that due to this impediment, the transportation cost of commuting to these suburban jobs becomes cost prohibitive, leaving black males with limited options of employment. In contrast, white males being present in the areas where these job opportunities are located do not have the obstacle of transportation cost. Therefore, white males' jobs prospects are plentiful and ever increasing.

To correct some of the issues illustrated by the spatial mismatch hypothesis, the government introduced the Gautreaux Assisted Housing Program which was a compromise born from a lawsuit filed against the Chicago Housing Authority in 1966. From this agreement, residents of the CHA were given section 8 certificates which would allow them to solicit housing anywhere in the metropolitan area. The government was obligated to pay a portion of the rent up to a stated amount. The program reached out to landlords also for their participation and involvement into the program. By 1981 after the initial test period, the program was rolled out to the remainder of the country and has been in force ever since.

This solution, however, has never solved the fundamental issue of employment disappearance in the urban areas. In the following section of this book, we will discuss in detail further answers to solving this urban dilemma, which by the way has been improving as city leaders have been making a conscious effort to revitalize inner ghetto areas. Still, it is sufficient to say here that these problems continue to persist and has created not a cycle of poverty but a *chain of events* which continues to draw African Americans back down into their *place*. America cannot move on until these links to the slave master past are broken and African Americans are not artificially sabotaged by the system and a false belief structure. The shackles which were supposedly removed six or seven generations ago have to be completely detached and forgotten; but as we wait for this *mountaintop*, we must develop both governmental and individual programs which will rehabilitate the thousands of African American males that we are now holding in prisons across the country. All our futures depend on everyone's success.

How can African Americans uplift America?

Dr. King spoke and wrote extensively about the uplifting of the Negro and through this process America will be brought into the *Promised Land*. I believe this is the essential message which he was trying to leave as his legacy. Plainly, Dr. King was challenging all Americans to overcome their internal prejudices and by emboldening African Americans with the rights each citizen holds very dear, African Americans through their empowerment can inspire America to reach its true greatness and attain its future prosperity. Whether I believe myself African American or not, I know my future, as all Americans, is tied to the successes and failures of all groups in America. This is the uniqueness and genius of the American system. The majority and minority groups must work together to arrive at a consensus which is in the best interest of our nation. Each group needs to have a voice in the direction of America. Only through the growth and improvements of all groups can America achieve its promise. If groups continue to squabble over their petty differences, America will never be able to lead the world to the *mountaintop*.

African Americans represent an inimitable test of American resolve and conviction in the systems and institutions which were conceived by our founding fathers. It is easy to accept a person to our shores who begged to enter and is similar to the people who are already here. However, can white Americans be so true of heart and soul to believe unwaveringly in their system of government and way of life that they will accept a group of people who has every reason to despise everything America has done for most of its history, because they were forced to be here, treated like property and sold like cattle? In turn, can that group see beyond the atrocities which they were required to endure and embrace the great promise that this country proclaims it believes above all else? If America is able to incorporate this group and give them the ability to pursue their happiness, then America will truly be the greatest nation on the face of the earth. They will assume their rightful place leading the world into the centuries which are to come. Americans can stand tall knowing that their system really is the most advanced form of democracy conceived by man, capable of bringing together all of mankind. If America continues to flounder and fail, they would leave to their children a system of broken promises and unfulfilled dreams.

Dr. King, I believe, prophetically foresaw this destination as the *Promised Land,* where America instills in everyone *the inalienable right to Life, Liberty and the Pursuit of Happiness.* Every person would be allowed to use their God given skills and provided the chance to achieve any heights to which those talents could take them. They would only be limited by their imagination and the fortitude of their desire to reach for all their dreams; nothing in America would be an artificial obstacle to their pursuits. As restated many times, in Dr. King's America it would not matter the *color of their skin*, merely the *content of their character,* thus enabling all kids the possibility to aspire to their full potential.

There are those who plainly fear this destiny. They simply do not believe that America will be able to maintain its hegemon dominance over the rest of the world. Those Americans hold the opinion that without white Europeans controlling the reins of power, America will not continue to lead the world in innovation and advancements. Furthermore, they cling to the notion that the growth in America is a product of the individual accomplishments of white Europeans charging ahead with an entrepreneurial spirit which they brought to the shores of the United States. They give little credence to the fact that although immigrants do come to America with a drive to succeed, the American system fosters this force and nurtures those individuals, providing them the opportunities to reach their goals. Basically, if it was solely the individual why did they have to come to America to fulfill their aspirations; why could they not have just obtained their dreams in their country of origin? It is quite grandiose to believe that the greatest governmental system ever conceived had little to do with one's success, and stupidly narcissistic to say that "*government played no role, I did it all on my own.*"

White immigrants were the first to take advantage of the system established by our forefathers; black people and other minority immigrants merely want the chance which was given to those white Europeans fleeing their countries; an opportunity to pursue their personal happiness without obstacles of racism and bigotry placed in their way. America is not a *zero sum gain*; the success of one group does not take from the accomplishments of another. Clearly, it is the opposite; the growth of one group enhances the achievements of all groups. African Americans have waited patiently for America to realize and live up to their creed, "*All men are created equal.*" America has no time to waste; it will forever be judged by how African Americans are treated, because, as many have conveniently forgotten from our history, their accomplishments set the tone for the future of America.

To move forward, America has to find equilibrium where societal barriers are removed and African Americans are personally inspired to follow their dreams and goals, like all immigrant groups which have come before. Dr. King fought to legally lower all the burdens that hinder the path to equality, and he, through his own experiences and achievements, stood as a role model to all Negroes, demonstrating that a Negro could reach the *mountaintop* without diminishing the value of those around him. African Americans cannot wait any longer for America to fulfill its promise; they must in this *age of individualism* seize the moment and through their initiative overcome the roadblocks which stand in their direction.

Dr. King supplied the blueprint which would empower African Americans, and furnish them the opportunity to achieve their *American dream.* In his early life, Dr. King valued family, faith and education. As he matured, he used this strong foundation to focus his attention on the pragmatic issues of his day, such as voting rights, economic inequality and segregation. African Americans should follow this path, starting with building their fundamental strengths, such as family structure and education, and then armed with these internal powers which are derived from their fortitude, demand changes in the practical policies that necessitate alteration like judicial bias, unequal employment opportunities, housing discrimination, disenfranchisement, and inadequate health care; accordingly, they will be able to solidify the future of generations to come.

To begin foundation construction, African Americans must tackle the problems associated with reinforcing the family unit. The family structure is the central element necessary to build a strong core, and as outlined in the previous section, the destruction of the family is the root of many issues in the African American community. Initially, we must modify social safety net programs which promote the separation of the family, and also solely are there to capture the desperately poor before the hit rock bottom. Our welfare state, as President Clinton attempted to do but was unable, should encourage the movement from welfare to work; however, it has to do so by taking into account the needs of all adults and children in the situation, basically, focusing on an integrated portfolio of solutions for each family, instead of this cookie-cutter approach which we are taking now. First, identifying and assessing the needs and requirements of each family and then through recommendation establish a comprehensive plan to resolve the issues present in the household. We should bring together all the social services in conjunction to find resolutions to the problems which plague a family, because piecemealing solutions to troubles are leaving many unresolved issues.

Some will argue the cost of implementing such a comprehensive approach will be astronomical, though losses in tax dollars from these families and the lack of productivity from the parents and the children would more than make up for the price tag of these services. Additionally, we are probably spending more presently on the individual social services that a typical family requires, when we take into consideration the overlapping services already being provided, with minimal results. Every dollar we invest in bringing a family away from the perils of poverty will sufficiently create returns which will multiply our principal investment. Programs such as Head Start for children and occupational job training for adults produce a significant return on our initial expenditure, and through early involvement we can considerably improve a family's ability to escape poverty.

From the Office of Planning, Research & Evaluation (OPRE), a study published in 2012 using data from students starting in the fall of 2009 found Head Start students who began below the national average in reading and writing showed significant improvement by the spring of 2010. This progression was well above peers of the same age. The data demonstrated this improvement by using a national mean of 100; Head Start students in the fall scored 96.4 and by the spring had achieved a 102.2 on the same scale. In addition to cognitive development, Head Start promotes family involvement in the process. Of the 1.3 million volunteers, 867,000 were parents who had children in the program. The families are encouraged to participate and enhance the learning process of the children, so by the spring of 2010, 77% of Head Start families reported reading to their child at least three times a week, and 92% were reviewing letters, words and numbers with their students. Lastly, the program tries to promote positive health development of the children. The study found that 98% of the children were active in daily outdoor sports and recreational activities, and 97% were covered by health insurance which emphasized well visits. Not so impressive, only 42% of families were eating fruits and vegetables twice on a daily basis.

For adults, work training programs have similar results. From the US Department of Labor (DOL), Employment & Training Administration, the Workforce Investment Act of 1998 signed by President Clinton has had measurable improvements in the functioning and efficacy of federal training programs. The DOL has been able to streamline the process for states and municipalities, allowing them to focus their attentions on the transition and retention of adult and dislocated workers. Even though the program received less funding than they got in 2006, the DOL has produced continually better results. In 2009, 685,903 adults and dislocated workers entered the workforce after completing the training and as of 2011 over 1 million had done so, which represented a 71.2% employment rate, with an 84.2% retention rate. Incredibly, the six month average earning for the combined group of adult and dislocated workers was over 13.9 billion dollars.

Although these programs are not perfect, they attempt to rectify the inequality in education and the job market by providing services which invest in our greatest resource, our people. For African Americans, these programs represent a way to break the *chain of events* which lead back to a torrid past. African Americans make up about one third of participants, so these programs are extremely important to their community. These programs are merely the beginning of the conversation. In this age of individualism, critics are correct that individual responsibility cannot be overlooked, but without societal and social rewards established to effectively endorse these behaviors continuous application of these actions will be short in duration. Specifically, if America does not provide the opportunity and ability to prosper from these training or education programs, their future participation levels shall suffer. The growth of economic opportunity in urban areas must be a focus of our public policy.

William Julius Wilson, author of <u>When Work Disappears</u>, looked to Japan and Germany for some of the answers for building employment options in inner cities. Although he was not implying that there was a direct correlation between European or Asian urban areas and those found in America, he simply argued that there are policies and techniques which we can learn from their experiences. In both urban areas, Wilson recognized the decline in low wage jobs stating that many have paid attention to blaming the supply side of the labor market, calling for personal accountability. However, most of the critics neglected to examine the demand side of the labor market to identify why private firms are refusing to hire low and non skilled workers, especially black workers. In these countries Wilson discovered that through public investment and infrastructure rehabilitation spending in urban areas, governments were able to create jobs and stimulate economic activities resulting in substantial economic and social growth. Economists Sheldon Danziger and Peter Gottschalk, in their book, <u>America Unequal</u>, further advocated the creation of labor-intensive minimum wage public service jobs to restructure and modernize inner city ghettoes, and perform duties that strapped city governments can no longer perform. Within these programs, we could also recognize workers who could be trained for higher level employment.

For the advocates like Bill Cosby and Juan Williams who still point to personal accountability as the key to correcting the ailments in the African American community, I concur that individual responsibility must be a part of any solution, but I would strongly argue even with everyone being a *Good Negro,* doing the right thing, segregation and lynchings to put Negroes *back in their place* would still have occurred. That being said, it is vital for the development of the family that African American males do take the personal responsibility for their children. The duties of fatherhood simply begin with conception, they do not end there. Over the last twenty years, ever since the Bradley Amendment in 1986, where as soon as child support becomes past due a non-expiring lien is placed on the obligated party, collection of child support has been relentless and effective. But it should not be necessary for fathers to be hunted down in order for them to own up to their responsibilities. Moreover, the portion of the law which recommends imprisonment for failure to pay obligation helps no one in the situation, it merely feeds into our nation's overzealousness to put "males" in jail.

Obviously, financial support for children is only a part of being a father; African American children are in need of the strong male role models for which African American males can provide. Young males of today confront many of the same issues faced by past generations; for instance, limited economic opportunities and varying forms of discrimination. Older African American males might provide guidance from their own experiences which should inspire youth to improve their own situations, and not merely remake the mistakes of yesterday. Most importantly, African American males can illustrate to their offspring the necessity to set their expectations higher than the accomplishments of their previous ancestors, melding like other immigrant groups which advanced their ethnic assimilation one generation at a time.

African American females must also take accountability for their actions, and build their family units by making choices which better fit their personal interest. While they are most frequently the unsung heroes, being left to nurture and raise their children in the absence of a family support system, African American females have to care for their own futures and unfulfilled lives with an untiring determination that they are *obligated* to their personal happiness and only *responsible* for the well being of others. They are too often placed in a position of obligatory servitude where they are made to believe that to be a *good woman* they must forgo their personal needs and desires. This societal and cultural pressure places African American females at a disadvantage with respect to their ability promote their own prosperity, in both the job markets and academic arenas.

Furthermore, those who are demanding more personal responsibility should be required to provide support for the most important developmental area for an African American which is the acceptance of education as a highly valued aspiration. Although leaders of the past have had varying attitudes towards the eventual use and content of education, they all agreed that education was vital to prevail over the repression which African Americans have dealt with for decades. As seen through history the limiting of education has been a method of control used by slave masters and southern whites to confine blacks to their secondary status. Consequently, we must emphasize education to break the chains which hold African Americans back from achieving their destinies.

In John McWhorter's book, <u>Losing The Race,</u> he discusses the idea that blacks are underachieving in schools because they suffer from what he calls *Anti-Intellectualism*. He believes that blacks portray themselves as victims and exhibit the stages that relate to that victimology, such as Separatism, which then leads to this overall "*black cultural*" phenomenon of *anti-intellectualism*. To reinforce his argument McWhorter uses singular examples of students who have underperformed, and draws the conclusion that their underperformance was a product of the resentment towards white establishment and their association with the school system. I truly do not know where to begin on how inaccurate this assessment of the black educational condition is. The only reason I included it in my book was to emphasize the amazing amount of ridiculous information which is on the market.

First, there is no overall black culture; is there an overall white culture? Black people even in Africa come from many different tribes and areas which follow distinctly different traditions and belief systems. To bundle everyone together and say they all bear ailments from the experiences of one group of black people is like saying every white person suffers from being a victim because Jews went through the Holocaust, and that would be completely unrealistic.

Second, the simplicity of the argument is laughable. I know many people want to believe that African Americans brought their entire situation upon themselves; however, it is just not true. White Americans, not all white people but quite a few, have perpetuated the situation by continuously trying to maintain African Americans in a submissive position. Education is the quintessential example and method used to sustain that dominance. Slave masters passed laws outlawing the education of slave because they knew that through education slaves could band together and overcome their tyranny. Slaves would become aware of their rights, and demand to be treated like people and not cattle. Hence, is it not plausible that southern whites and other whites who wanted to keep African Americans as second class citizens would use lack of education as a means of bondage?

Lastly, African Americans, contrary to popular belief, have never as an overall group acted like victims. They have generation after generation constantly fought and struggled against overwhelming forces which have unrelentingly constructed roadblocks and barriers in their way, but still they have persisted onward towards the "*Promised land.*" Even today, as lawmakers in states all over the country are trying to disproportionately hinder the education of black people through underfunding and lack of resources, the fight to educate black youth is required to continuously be waged, as if they are receiving something they do not deserve, or as McWhorter is implying they do not want. America needs the productivity of black youths going into the future, forgetting about them or wishing they merely disappear will not solve the problems.

Bad curriculum, poor teachers and inadequate resources acted as a form of shackles which branded African American students with the label of underachievers, and limited African Americans from advancing beyond the boundary of second class citizen. Although there is a portion of individual responsibility which ought to be considered by the African American community, as stated earlier, much of the blame for the failing public school system resides squarely on the shoulders of white civic leaders who have chosen to disregard the development of these disadvantaged students. Moreover, even with the decision of *Brown v. Board of Education,* these leaders have for all intents and purposes maintained segregated school systems in many areas of the country, especially inner cities.

To solve these perpetual problems in our school systems, William Julius Wilson looked to foreign examples for some guidance. He found the key to resolving most of the problems is an equal distribution of resources to all public schools across the entire nation. The government should not permit any public school to fall below a baseline level of resources. A school in the inner city of Chicago should not have significantly less capability than a school in Greenwich, Connecticut. Much of this is done through public and private partnerships, where public resources and private donations are pooled in order to facilitate better school conditions. Wilson also found that European students are graduating high school with skill that are necessary for immediate entry into the job market unlike here in America, where students are not acquiring these same skills until after college. Consequently, a more practically based curriculum through the earlier years of schooling would definitely be more beneficial in educating all students, particularly African Americans.

From the book, The Covenant with Black America, hereafter referred to as the *Covenant*, the authors outlined common sense solutions to the problems which trouble the school system. These solutions demanded both individual responsibility and societal changes in both attitude and policy in order to resolve the issues which plague our schools. The *Covenant* outlines what individual parents and care takers of students must do to instill a love for learning and help their children get sufficiently prepared for the challenges of school. The most important thing is for parents to get involved in their child's learning process, by reading to them, establishing a clean quiet area for them to do their homework, checking their homework, so they know you are monitoring, and becoming involved in the school activities. Parents need to have a firsthand knowledge of what is going on in their kids' school and community. This will allow parents to hold leaders and elected officials accountable for the policies and results in the school.

The *Covenant* goes on to outline the responsibilities of leaders and elected officials. First, officials must invest in the children and the parents in these communities. Local officials have to create a holistic plan of enrichment including afterschool programs with the expectations that the students will be prepared for either a college or a trade school upon graduation of secondary school. The officials should further find methods to engage the parents in establishing these expectations and for those parents who, because of work commitments, cannot physically attend conferences or progress meetings, other means of communications like conference calls and email could be utilized. Second, the federal government should ensure that all children have access to pre-school education and Head Start programs. Studies indicate that these programs give unprivileged children a means of equalizing their initial disadvantages. Finally, the government at all levels, must work together and coordinate their actions so they can provide adequate resources, in terms of minimal class sizes and sufficient pay for teachers and a universal curriculum which ensures students from all regions of the country will have similar experiences.

In summary, the *Covenant* and Mr. Wilson both show strategies which hinge on private and public participation in the educational process. These groups have to engage resources in early stages of the educational career of disadvantaged students. Each resolution depends on the involvement of parents and other adults in the lives of students, helping children have a voice in their futures. Parents and stake holding adults must exercise their civic duty and demand of elected officials that they perform their responsibility for each child, leaving, as President Bush wanted, *No Child Left Behind*. But America has to make a better commitment than they did under the *No Child Left Behind* program to save every student.

In addition, one of important components of a student's developmental process is the establishment of a self. African Americans have struggled with the formulation of an identity because of the orchestrated efforts made by slave masters and southern whites. As Frederick Douglass articulated, *"He met very few slaves that even knew their own birthday"*; consequently, the oppressors destroyed any knowledge of who slaves were and where they came from. As a result, African American children do not have their family trees to use as a reference point for understanding their personal strengths and weaknesses, like other immigrant groups who can draw strength from the past ancestors to overcome their present impediments. Identifying these individual assets and liabilities of student will empower students to reach further and overcome the obstacles in their path.

If we take a common method of personality testing used by corporate America to understand the strengths and weaknesses of their employees, we can isolate assets and liabilities which could begin to fill the gaps in self identification which is missing in many African Americans. These assessments could be utilized early and later in development to help those students which indicate a need for corrective intervention. Then through portfolio learning principles, specific areas of weakness of a child's development can be focused upon and improved while increasing his/her enthusiasm towards learning by building on personal strengths. The later use of these assessments possibly will discover areas of strong potential which can be utilized to introduce vocational areas of interest, helping students find a direction which might lead to future employment and success.

Through implementation of these programs, African Americans would build family and educational foundations which provide the basis for expanding upon Dr. King and the civil rights movements' journey for societal changes. These modifications in American culture will then give African Americans a true opportunity to get closer to the *Promised Land*. Although the civil rights acts have been updated numerous times attempting to outlaw discrimination, oppressors have circumvented the laws and pursued avenues of prejudice which are outside the perimeters of the legislations.

For instance, judicial bias was not addressed by any legislation; however, it is obvious that since the end of slavery, it is more likely for an African American male to be put in prison than it is for any other males from different ethnicities. As outlined early, African Americans make up a disproportionate percentage of the prison population, which is having detrimental consequences for African Americans as a whole. The so called *War on Drugs* and mandatory sentencing guidelines have given jurisdictions the chance to profile and incarcerate African Americans on a seemingly nondiscriminatory basis. As discussed, this imprisonment of young and adult men is having deep and lasting effects on the African American community for generations to come.

The *Covenant* illustrates possible solutions to this covert form of discrimination. The African American community is required to do more to keep their kids away from the path of the drug dealers and petty thieves, meaning that they have to try and provide children with an appreciation for all the options which are available to them. In the absence of this parental guidance church and civic leaders should attempt to show these opportunities are within their grasp. The setting of expectations throughout the entire community where all African Americans expect outstanding achievement in both athletics and education will enable everyone to play a significant role in raising and fostering their children.

Nevertheless, even with complete participation from the community, without changes in the drug laws, which presently target minor drug dealers and addicts, carrying mandatory sentences, and stricter judicial oversight, the African American community will continue to suffer from this blatant injustice. The *Covenant* emphasizes a few different ways that elected officials could stem the tide of an unequal judicial system. First, the officials should change the war on drugs to more of a crusade to get the users help and rehabilitation through substance abuse treatment programs. An investment in curing the addictions would be a better use of our resources than immediately resorting to incarceration. Some states initiated programs which provide addicts court-supervised substance abuse treatments, as opposed to prison sentences. Once offenders complete these programs, the charges for possession would be dismissed.

Second, elected officials have to put an end to mandatory sentencing, giving magistrates the discretion to determine the best course of action for any particular defendant in a drug case. Many drug cases for minor offenses, such as possession or small dealing, carry immediate prison sentencing for offenders. Also, since police in exorbitantly disproportionate numbers are arresting and profiling black males for these offenses, thousands of males are being jailed on a regular basis, leading to excessive incarceration totals. Judges could better determine whether the offenders and the society would be served if other solutions were found.

Finally, the *Covenant* outlines that the juvenile justice system must be examined and improved to correct for perpetuating the career criminal. Juveniles have to be provided multiple opportunities to rehabilitate their lives, so that they can become productive participants in society. It is necessary for lawmakers to establish grant programs, job training and emotional counseling for ex-offenders in order for them to have avenues which lead away from a life of crime and drugs. The leaders of the African American community and policy-makers must join together to illuminate alternatives to an impoverished way of life which does not include drugs or criminal activities. It is the responsibility of everyone to put these young people on the right track.

Some other areas which were not completely addressed by legislation are housing discrimination, workplace inequality, profiling, media bias, and health care disadvantages. However, without a change in the underlying premise that black people, particularly African Americans, are a sub-cultural, subservient group with common destructive characteristics, which is beneath the European white culture from which most white Americans hail, there can never be a systemic eradication of discrimination. Prejudice will continue to linger below the surface and blacks will have to continuously prove their worth in whatever endeavor or area of life they choose to enter. As in the case, *Florida v George Zimmerman,* the jury demanded that Trayvon Martin rise from the dead and dispute the facts that though he was profiled, followed, and confronted by a man with some police training, that being a seventeen year old black kid, he had the wherewithal to completely over power a twenty-eight year old man. When he could not be resurrected to tell his story, a white man was again allowed to kill a young black boy. Hence, an unarmed black child, since he is a *thug,* must be able to subdue a grown man. Would the bar be set so high for a skinny seventeen year old white kid?

This simple subconscious inference that a black child is somehow more developed than his white counterpart leads to caustic conclusions. As in this case, the jury concluded that this child did not need protecting from a 28 year old man; on the contrary, the 28 year old white man needed to be protected from this 17 year old black child. All these subconscious and covert beliefs about race differences can have detrimental consequences. In business and in life, some believe that black workers are less punctual and more likely to steal, so every black job applicant must overcome these inherent ideas in order to be considered for employment. Therefore, if hired, the black employee is accused first, and if something were to happen, fired first under suspicion. With respect to lending bias, lenders believe black borrowers are more likely to default, so blacks are given less latitude when hardship occurs, and higher lending costs in the beginning of the process. The preconceived notions that Americans have about race and the characteristics which are manifested from their beliefs cause discrimination in situations where conscious bigotry may not be present. Not until America begins to acknowledge this form of bias can solutions be found to truly eradicate inequality in our society.

Why is the future bright for blacks, especially African Americans?

Any group, who has persevered through slavery, lynchings, segregation, police brutality, and numerous other forms of discrimination and oppression, shall triumph over any challenges which confront them in the future. Many have questioned the fortitude of African Americans but they quickly forget how much generations after generations have had to tolerate and rise above in order to achieve their unprecedented number of advancements. African Americans have been the necessary catalysts who instigated the great internal struggle which will allow America to become a *more perfect union*. America can never reach its zenith without recognizing the errors of its past. It is overcoming these deficiencies that will make our trek such a rewarding adventure.

Dr. King led America on this journey towards the *mountaintop*. He called for the unification of Americans behind our creed, *"All Men are created Equal,"* and for the most part America has listened to that call. Blacks, especially African Americans, have their greatest opportunity since slavery to rise above the bondages of the slave masters and reach for the *American Dream*. The majority of Americans recognizes and admits to the mistaken beliefs of the past, and is open to the changing face of America.

This new face of America can be seen everywhere. Black, especially African American, successes are evident throughout our entire society. From athletic achievements which have translated to iconic media figures, to business moguls who have amassed empires, to finally a black man from humble beginnings who was able to aspire to the highest office in the land, black Americans' contributions to the fabric of the American society are being woven into every corner of our nation. Dr. King would have been proud to know that with every small step forward we are building an unobstructed path to the future for our children.

Nonetheless, Dr. King would still caution that our work is far from complete, and some one need not be black or African American to recognize that equality of all men which enables any person to pursue his happiness is the singular greatness of America. The inability of any American to pursue his *God given rights* threatens not only him but every other American, because there may come a time when those roadblocks that held a black man back could be erected to stop anyone's progress. America has to bravely move into the future without reservations or fear. We must simply have faith in the system and the people who call themselves Americans.

Critics would hold on tightly to the notion that America cannot survive with this changed face; the white face which made America great in the past is the only one that can continue the greatness into the future. The problem with their argument is that America is already changing into a nation with a different face

143

and the only thing stopping us from achieving our greatness are those who will not relinquish that false belief. They hold America's future hostage while they dream of yesterdays. America, as our history demonstrates, has always been a country of multiple faces and cultures, and many have merely hidden the other faces behind that white image. The only difference is that each one of those groups today wants to be counted. America's evolution will be complete when it can accept the existence of multi-cultural groups and differentiate between those groups, instead of trying to create bipolar enemies. We are all Americans and demand to be credited for building this nation.

Dr. King recognized that this journey would continue without him, and truthfully it will persevere regardless if any of us were here, because there would be others to take the place of those who fought so gallantly. This fact does not diminish their achievement it only demonstrates the enormity of their cause, how it goes beyond any individual. Many black Americans have played significant roles in this movement, some without even trying; they have simply quested for their *American Dreams* and were in their own way able to move the cause forward and upward towards the *mountaintop*.

One of these African Americans was Cassius Clay, later known as Muhammad Ali. Cassius Clay introduced the world to a black man who could captivate the white audiences as well as the black population. He simply transcended race lines and became a mega star in an era, when blacks faced discrimination down every path they chose to follow. Clay's silky tongue and lighting fast hands made him a natural entertainer, which gave all those who followed the ability to walk in the path he paved.

Born January 17, 1942, Cassius Marcellus Clay, Jr. grew up in Louisville, Kentucky, son of a father with the same name, who was a billboard and sign painter, and mother, Odessa O'Grady Clay, who was a domestic servant. Cassius had a typical childhood for a youth growing up in the segregated south. He attended all black schools and spent most of his time with solely black children and adults. He, however, recognized that many of the black children around him wanted to be white, so they could have the privileges of the white children. He knew from a young age that this was not his wish; he would do something which would someday help his people. Cassius merely did not know yet what God's plan was for him.

Then on a fateful night in October, 1954, when he was twelve years old, after attending a merchandise exposition for black patrons, he exited the arena just to notice that his "*red and white Schwinn*" bicycle had been stolen. Furious, he vowed to find the thief and give him a proper "*whupping*." Half-crying, he met Joe Martin, a local police officer, who also taught boxing in his off hours. Joe told him, "Well, you better learn how to fight before you start challenging people that you're gonna whup." From that night forward Cassius Clay, Jr.'s life would be changed forever.

Over the next few years, Cassius was not a very good student. He scored an 83 on the Standard California Intelligence Quotient Test, and struggled through school, but found his salvation in the ring. He won 108 amateur bouts, winning six Kentucky Golden Gloves championships, two National Golden Gloves tournaments, and two National AAU titles. Still, to most of the nation, Cassius Clay was a relative unknown, but that all changed when Cassius won the 1960 Olympic Gold Medal against the three time European champion and Bronze Medal winner from Poland. In that fight, Cassius found his style of quick short jabbing, and immediately backing off so he could not get hit, always bouncing on his toes.

Cassius's Olympic gold performance made him a hero in the black community and an instant celebrity to all other Americans. He was the perfect combination of qualities; he was young, handsome, charismatic, entertaining, and incredibly gifted. Cassius embraced the limelight and *"radiated the aura of an All-American boy."* He, above all else, seemingly fed off any crowd that gathered and loved to continually do a stand up performance anywhere he went. One of his signature routines was his ability to make up poems for every occasion. Consequently, upon his arrival at Louisville Airport to joyous crowd, Cassius recited his first published poem:

How Cassius Took Rome

To Make America the greatest is my goal,
So I beat the Russian, and I beat the Pole,
And for the USA won the Medal of Gold.
Italians said, "You're greater than the Cassius of Old."

We like your name, we like your game,
So make Rome your home if you will.
I said I appreciate your kind hospitality,
But USA is my country still,
'Cause they waiting to welcome me in Louisville."

There were people from all over wanting to be the manager of this new sensation. They all promised that they would provide the best training and promotion for the future champion. He and his parents finally agreed to sign with the Louisville Sponsoring Group which gave him a $10,000 signing bonus and a very attractive contract that also set up a pension for his retirement. As a result, on October 29, 1960, Cassius Clay, Jr. with tremendous fanfare became a professional fighter. In build up to the first fight, Cassius's flamboyant personality stole the show. The fight was against Tunney Hunsaker, who was a part-time fighter. Cassius won the fight in a six round decision.

As Cassius Clay's career exploded, he opened the door for all fighters to collect much more lucrative purses. The Sponsoring Group protected their investment by making sure that Cassius received the best training from the most renowned boxers in the country. After being turned down by the great Sugar Ray Robinson, who was still hoping to lengthen his career, the Group hired Angelo Dundee, an experienced boxing coach and trainer. Dundee became much more than a trainer for Cassius, they established a lifelong friendship.

By the Archie Moore fight, Cassius was drawing huge crowds to his fights. Archie Moore had been one of Cassius's many trainers early in his career, but needed to sign on to this

147

fight in order to pay off some debts which were hounding him. Leading up to the fight Cassius again put on a show, antagonizing Moore for the crowds which gathered for their weigh-in and promotional events. On the night of the fight, 16,200 fans paid over $182,600 to see the fight. This box office revenue was the largest amount ever collected to witness an indoor bout. The fight was dubbed the *"Battle of the Century"* by Arthur Daley of the *New York Times*. Cassius knocked Moore out in the fourth round and his journey to the title was underway.

Cassius Clay's popularity was growing by leaps and bounds. It seemed silly that no fighter before had seen the fighting game as entertainment, but Cassius Clay was now an entertainment icon crossing lines where no one had ventured to traverse before. In 1963, as a marketing stunt, Cassius released an album of his greatest monologues and poems. Although the album had only moderate commercial success, it significantly grew the marketability of the Cassius Clay brand. He was known to a new audience who did not necessarily appreciate boxing.

Cassius's iconic rise climaxed on February 25, 1964, when Clay met the Heavyweight Champion of the World, Sonny Liston, named one of the top 15 greatest punchers of all time. In the seventh round, Cassius Clay knocked out Liston and became the new Heavyweight champion; he had reached another of his childhood goals. Though he had achieved the pinnacle of his dreams, he was still missing something. He was one of the first extremely successful black men in the white world. But he felt that he had not accomplished the childhood desire of making a difference for his people. To achieve this goal he turned to a fellow media superstar at the time, Malcolm X.

Malcolm recruited Cassius to join his organization the Nation of Islam. Cassius had always had an interest in Islam and the teachings of Allah. At first Elijah Muhammad did not allow Cassius to join because of his propensity to violence indicated by his boxing career, but with the notoriety of his career, and he was now the Heavyweight champion, Muhammad knew Cassius would bring immediate publicity to the Nation. Muhammad almost immediately did away with Cassius's slave name and renamed him Muhammad Ali.

The white media went into a frenzy on the news that the "*good boy*," Cassius Clay had joined the Black Muslims, and now wanted to be known as Muhammad Ali. All the media knew of the Nation was that they believed white people were evil, and the blacks in the organization thought they were superior. Ali felt he had found his means of helping his people. This move to Islam was fated by God; it was his destiny. He studied the writings of Elijah Muhammad, and any books that Muhammad recommended him to read. He also attracted other popular athletes to join movements to encourage black power, for instance, the show of protest which occurred at the Olympics in 1968.

As his popularity was plummeting in the white community, his status among blacks and even around the world, especially in Africa, was growing. Then, the biggest test of his faith and resolve came when he was drafted in 1965 to enlist in the Vietnam War. After not responding to his name being called three times, Ali told the draft board that he was not participating in the war on the grounds that the Vietcong had not called him *"Nigger."* The draft officials arrested him and a court sentenced him to five years in prison and a $10,000 fine. Ali appealed the case all the way to the Supreme Court. While waiting for review, he was stripped of his title, and no state licensing body would allow him to fight.

During his exile, Muhammad Ali was a lightning rod for the growing anti-war movement. He was given many opportunities to speak at colleges all over the country. His popularity as spokesman for the changing social discourse and the evolving political environment gave him a new status which few in the society have ever attained. By 1971, the majority of Americans had joined the anti-war faction and the Supreme Court overturned his conviction, on the grounds the war violated his freedom of religion. With this decision he could restart his boxing career. He wanted to go after the title he felt was rightfully his.

There was another young fighter on the scene, who was dominating the heavyweight division; his name was Joe Frazier, the new darling of the white establishment. Joe Frazier had destroyed fighters in his four title defenses, and was just waiting for Ali to make his way back. Joe wished to step in the ring with Ali because he wanted to be known as the best ever, and without defeating Ali that would never happen.

Finally, the fight was signed. Ali-Frazier was dubbed the "*Fight of the Century,*" and the fighters agreed to the largest purse in history. Each fighter was to take home $2.5 million. Madison Garden provided the majority of the $5 million guaranteed purse. A purse this large was completely unprecedented, but if the fighters had opted to take the original offer which consisted of a split of $1.25 million and 35% of the pay per view and door revenues, each fighter would have received approximately nine million dollars. In a fifteen round unanimous decision, Frazier defeated Ali marking the first defeat in Ali's career.

Ali's quest to regain the title was impeded, though only for a brief moment, because in the rematch Ali was able to beat Frazier to become the undisputed Heavyweight Champion. But his role as an American icon had transcended the arena of sports; he had become a black leader in the political debates of the time and in the social arguments which were permeating throughout the nation. Although his transition to Islam did for a period, intimidate the white establishment and probably decreased his popularity in the long run, his magnetic personality and incredible abilities enabled him to maintain a status of media superstar, giving him the legendary standing of the "Greatest". Thus, Muhammad Ali was able to construct the groundwork for future black athletes, performers and political candidates which built off the foundation that Ali provided.

The next major icon that rose from the underpinnings of Muhammad Ali to reshape the status of the African American

151

athlete and man, in general, was Michael Jordan. Other athletes, like Magic Johnson and Jim Brown, catapulted the image of the black athlete, but no one changed the portrait of the black man more than Michael, the darling of Madison Avenue. Michael brought the face of a black man into the living rooms and kitchens of households all over America and the world. He made every child and many adults want to buy his products in order to *"Be like Mike."*

Born February 17, 1963 in Brooklyn, New York to James R. and Deloris Jordan, the family moved to Wilmington, North Carolina when Michael was very young, where the Jordan's raised their 5 children. Michael Jeffrey Jordan, also known as MJ, was the fourth of the five children. He had two older brothers and an older sister and younger sister. Being the baby boy, Michael wanted to do everything his older brothers did. This instilled in him an incredible undaunting competitive drive.

This spirit drove Michael to play baseball, football, and basketball. He excelled at all three sports, throwing a record 45 innings of no hit baseball. Moreover, Michael, unfortunately, was slow to spurt, as he was only 5'10" when he tried out for the varsity basketball team as a sophomore at Emsley A. Laney High School. Coach Clifton "Pops" Herring was looking for taller and more experienced players to fill his varsity squad, so coach cut Michael, and kept his much taller friend, Leroy Smith, who was the sole sophomore to make varsity because he was 6'7". Herring was trying out 50 boys for the 15 varsity spots and 15 junior varsity positions, and posted the results of the tryouts on 2 separate lists in the gymnasium. Michael ran home and cried that night when he did not see his name on the varsity list, and his friend, Leroy, was there. This was Michael first encounter with failure, which changed him forever. Leroy stated later that Michael was wildly competitive before but now the cut made him insanely determined to never let it happen again.

The jayvee games became a fan attraction, even the varsity players would show up early to see Michael play. He averaged 26 points per game, and put on a show for the crowd. By the following year, Michael had grown four inches and was now a bonafide star at the school. Over his next two years, he received McDonald All-American honors and scholarship offers from numerous Division 1 basketball powerhouses. Michael chose to attend University of North Carolina Tar Heels with famed Hall of Fame coach Dean Smith. He originally wanted to attend UCLA, but they failed to recruit him, and he picked UNC over UNC State because he liked Coach Smith.

While Coach Smith played a team oriented game, Michael immediately made an impact on the program. His outstanding work ethic and determination to never fail again made him push himself and his teammates at practice. Michael accomplished a feat very rarely done, which was to start as a freshman on a Dean Smith coached team. Michael won freshman Player of the Year in the Atlantic Coast Conference. UNC was the preseason favorite to win the national championship, but had to compete with fellow perennial basketball power Georgetown, led by Patrick Ewing. With 15 seconds to go, Michael hit a 16 foot jump shot which lifted UNC over Georgetown for the National Championship and the celebration began. Although Michael did not win another national championship, in the next two years he made both All American teams and in his junior year he won national Player of the Year. By the end of his junior year the NBA was knocking and his draft stock was extremely high. During that summer, Michael won the first of his two Gold medals.

Teams were salivating waiting for the opportunity to draft basketball's next expected superstar. However, Michael was again pushed back by height. Two centers, Hakeem Olajuwon and Sam Bowie, were taken as the first two players in the draft, so Michael fell to the third spot. The Chicago Bulls selected Michael with that third pick and his NBA dream had begun. Michael brought the same no nonsense tenacity to both the practices and the games; similar to how he had done since missing the cut in high school. But Michael was no longer the relative unknown; he was the man everyone came to see. The Bulls were a perennially bad team with small crowds coming to the arena. In a relatively short time Michael changed the expectations and the atmosphere around the Bulls. People started to flock to the games, and the league was buzzing with this new phenomenon out of North Carolina. Even on the road Michael was drawing huge crowds into opponents' venues. He was growing the brand of the NBA;

Michael alone accounted for $10 billion in revenues for the NBA over his career.

Michael's popularity was growing in all segments of the population; whether white or black everyone was astonished with Mike's abilities. Michael's agent, David Falk, set up a meeting with Nike and their CEO Phil Knight. Nike was looking for a new spokesman to endorse their basketball shoes, but Michael and his parents went to the meeting with reservation because he had never really worn Nike. Michael loved Adidas and he wore Converse all through college. But Nike was offering him what no one had ever offered a player before, his own shoe and clothing line, with an endorsement deal which could be worth hundreds of millions of dollars. Before this deal Nike had basically only given players $10,000 to endorse their shoes. Both sides were entering into a partnership which was a complete leap of faith. The relationship would forever change the way advertisements would be viewed and make Michael a megastar.

Not even those at the table envisioned the incredible success that would come from the campaign; Nike executives had estimated that in 3 or 4 years they could expect $3 million in gross sales. The conventional wisdom was that unlike Muhammad Ali, a team player could not be marketed as an individual and move people to follow him like a cult. However, Michael's play on the court was extraordinary and his relentless work ethic propelled him to legendary status. He won Rookie of the Year, and received more fan votes to the All-Star game than any other player in the league. He was becoming a fan favorite, even though the other veteran players did not appreciate the publicity this rookie was getting, and in some reports the veterans collaborated to snub him at the All-Star game.

By the time the first Nike campaign hit the airways, it was obvious this was going to be a mammoth success. The new Air Jordan line of footwear exploded on the market, and Michael was extremely comfortable in front of the camera. In 1985 it's reported that the Air Jordan line grossed $130 million in sales worldwide, after merely one year in mass production. Michael Jordan was on his way to becoming the most recognized person on the planet. The campaigns that ensued plastered Michael's face everywhere which raised Michael to iconic status.

Michael parlayed this media onslaught into endorsement deals with other major corporations such as McDonald's and Gatorade. The face of a black man entered everyone's living room whether they liked it or not. He presented to America a new image of a black man who was successful and popular beyond belief. A new generation of Americans wanted Air Jordan to drink Gatorade and to eat at McDonald, so they could be "*like Mike.*"

On the court, Michael was also taking the world by storm. After recovering from his broken foot which made him miss most of his second season, Michael came back his third year and scorched the league for 30 points per game, leading the NBA in scoring. Over the next few years, he won the league MVP,

Defensive Player of the Year and led the Bulls to the playoffs, but the NBA championship eluded him. Critics started to call him a selfish player, merely interested in his own stats to the detriment of the team. Tex Winter, an assistant coach with the Bulls said, referring to Jordan, *"There is no 'I' in team,"* to which Jordan replied, *"but there is in 'win'."*

To solve the lack of championships the Bulls began addressing the urgent need to put better players around Michael, and provide him a coach who could get Michael to see the value of the those players. In came Scotty Pippen and Phil Jackson. Scotty Pippen was a dynamic player drafted out of University of Central Arkansas. Pippen was a strong defender, great passer and clutch scorer. He was literally the *"Robin"* to Jordan's *"Batman"*. Phil Jackson was a seasoned veteran player who saw the battles which went on in the trenches of the NBA, a successful coach from the "D" league, with little NBA coaching experience, but an incredible way of communicating with players. The stage was set for Michael to prove he could lead a team to the championship and quiet all his detractors.

The "Bad Boys" from Detroit, led by Isiah Thomas, who everyone believed was the master mind behind the snubbing of Michael at his first All-star game, stood in their way. After a heart wrenching defeat to the Pistons in 1990, where it was reported the Pistons used special plays they called *"Jordan Rules,"* the Bulls powered pass the Pistons in 1991 to win their first of three championships, defeating Magic Johnson's Los Angeles Lakers in 5 games.

Michael's status as the *"Greatest Basketball Player"* ever was solidified, and his tremendous fan base was growing exponentially. He built upon the groundwork already set by Muhammad Ali, where a new generation of Americans was comfortable with a black man on their television and selling their most used products. Although it was not Michael's intention to move the cause forward, his ability to connect with the audience, his charismatic personality, and his capability to appeal outside the arena of sports enabled him to push other blacks into the forefront of American society. Michael Jordan is the model for a new generation of successful black men, both in sports and business.

Jordan's iconic rise helped other black Americans to be accepted in other spheres of American society. Another pivotal person was General Colin Powell, who many believed when he first entered the scene as the leader of the Joint Chiefs of Staff would be the first black president of the United States. General Powell's high profile leadership during the Gulf War and in his constant exposure through his other appointments in government, which occurred after, such as Secretary of State, broke the glass ceiling for black Americans, enabling Barack Hussein Obama to become President of the United States.

Colin Luther Powell, although not an African American, was born April 5, 1937 in Harlem, a neighborhood of Manhattan.

His parents, like mine, were first generation immigrants from Jamaica. Maud Ariel and Luther Theophilus Powell raised their two children, Colin and Marilyn, in the South Bronx in New York City, a very ethnically diverse area of the Bronx with a large extended Jamaican family which promoted the value of education to improve the lives of the next generation. Colin was a self proclaimed average student who was far behind many of his Jamaican relatives and friends. All through high school and in the beginning of college Colin could not truly find his passion for anything; he bounced around from different summer jobs and with minimal effort sustained his strong C average in most of his classes. Marilyn was the Powell who upheld the family dignity with respect to school.

With no true direction to his college career, having given up on engineering, Colin became enamored with the students on campus who were parading around in military uniforms. He viewed them as incredibly distinguished, exhibiting an image of honor. So in the fall of 1954, he decided to join the Reserved Officers Training Corps (ROTC). Almost immediately, he knew he had found his calling. He struggled through his math and physics classes; actually did well and enjoyed geology, but he looked forward to his ROTC program, both drills and classes. While receiving C's in most of his other academic areas of study, Colin was getting A's in all of his ROTC related work. He loved the discipline and pageantry of wearing the uniform.

159

His next three years passed by quickly, and college graduation was already here. His grades had improved over the years; he truly enjoyed geology, but his ROTC grades had inflated his average. Another stage of his life was about to begin, and Colin had to satisfy his obligation to the army. He looked forward to his opportunity to be an army officer, and he was ready to repay the army for his education; he owed the army a three year enlistment on active duty. Colin was ready to take on the new challenge of becoming a first lieutenant. His first assignment as a full time soldier was to go to Fort Benning in Georgia for basic training for officers, which would take five months to complete.

Before leaving for Georgia, Colonel Brookhart, who was the ROTC commander and had become very close to Colin, sat him down to discuss his deployment. He wanted Colin to understand that Georgia was in the Deep South and was not like New York. He articulated that Colin would be in a world he did not create and had no ability to change, so to go there and try to *"buck the system"* would merely get him into trouble. He told the story of a black General Benjamin O. Davis who tried to fight the system and got himself in a whole lot of trouble. In essence, the colonel was warning Colin to be a "Good Negro" and stay out of trouble. Colin took this advice with the sincerity in which it was given, and appreciated the colonel taking the time to deliver this message. Anyway, although he never really encountered much racism in his life, he felt he would not be distracted from his primary focus of becoming a good soldier.

The eight weeks of infantry training was followed by ranger training and then airborne training. Colin was exhausted, underweight and suffering from an infection in the leg, which he told no one about, because he did not want to fall behind his classmates. The army ROTC graduates were training alongside the cadets from WestPoint and they all got along very well. The training reinforced the notion that a soldier follows orders with no questions or ambiguity; there were absolutely no gray areas for deviation.

The racism in the Deep South was definitely different than the north, as the colonel had warned. The segregated society presented an obstacle, which Colin, who was relatively new to this type of blatant bigotry, had to quickly get accustomed. At times it made him feel hurt; sometimes he felt anger; however, most of the time he merely felt challenged, with an inner yearning to overcome and persevere. He was determined not to allow anything to distract him from his goal, regardless of how much he was provoked.

When the five months came to an end and the commencement ceremony for the new Airborne Rangers was finally here, Colin experienced an incredible feeling of accomplishment, and was ready to leave Georgia and return to Queens to see his family. He looked forward to his family seeing him in his uniform. He reveled in the idea that when he left Queens merely five months ago, he was an ordinary college graduate and now he had been transformed into an *"airborneranger ."* Like he had hoped, everyone had wonder and amazement in their eyes as they gazed at *"Colin! Airborne Ranger"*.

After a short period at home, he needed to report for his first position which would station him across the ocean in West Germany, where Colin would be able to finally be in the real army with actual army soldiers. Up until this point, he had merely been around officers in training not any enlisted personnel. He was ready to see the army from their point of view. Black soldiers relished in this assignment to Germany, especially those from the south. For the first time in their lives, they could drink where they wanted to; they could eat where they wanted to; and they could, most importantly, date who they wanted to. The Germans were extremely nice to American soldiers because they knew that these Americans stood between them and the *"Red hordes"* which marched on the other side of the wall.

There is always a dark side to any bright cloud, and Germany was no exception. Colin immediately became acutely aware of an infectious unhealthy attitude which was plaguing the entire chain of command, from the privates all the way up to the generals. At each level the entire garrison was willing to cut corners and lie in order to make it appear that the jobs were getting done and the objectives were being accomplished. These practices troubled Colin greatly, and in just a few years, *"this self-deception would be expanded, institutionalized, and exported with tragic results to Vietnam."* So much so, when it came time for his two tours of duty to come to an end, all he could do was find an immediate exit, even though his commanding officer urged him to sign up for another tour.

While in Germany, Colin had received his promotion to first lieutenant, which was automatic in eighteen months as long as a officer kept his nose clean and performed his duties. His next assignment would allow Colin to be closer to home, so he could see his family more. The duty was at Fort Devens located near Ayers, Massachusetts, about 30 miles west of Boston. In his first job as liaison officer, he was a *"gofer"* for Major Richard D. Ellison, who was in charge of operations and training for the battle group. This job was very short lived before Colin found a way to escape and become the executive officer of Company A, which made him the second in command. In a very brief time, the company commander was reassigned, and Colin assumed command. This was his second command in a very small amount of time in the army. He quickly learned the necessary *"tricks of the trade"* which ensured that his men had all the supplies they needed.

Fort Devens gave Colin a glimpse at what army life was going to be as he ascended up the chain of command, and his frequent opportunities to go back to Queens allowed him to see what life would be like for a black college graduate in civilian life. Although there were some benefits of civilian life, such as more freedom, a black officer in the army had a much more promising career. The army was further ahead on integrating the ranks than the civilian society. Therefore, Colin chose to re-enlist when his obligation was over. He wanted to pursue an army career.

Over the following year, Colin's career progressed and he met Alma Johnson, the daughter of a high school principal in Birmingham, Alabama. Alma was a very bright, beautiful, and proper southern girl who had skipped grades through school so she could graduate college at nineteen, and got her graduate degree in Audiology from Emerson College. Alma was an audiologist for the Boston Guild for the Hard of Hearing. Her job was to drive an audio van into poor areas and provide people with free hearing tests. Colin knew from the very first moment that Alma was very special.

Colin's stay at Fort Devens was coming to an end, and he was highly regarded by many of his commanders. He expected his orders any day. In August 1962, his orders arrived and he was being shipped to South Vietnam in order to become a military advisor. These deployments were only given to the select few who the army believed had a significant career ahead. Colin was ordered to report to Fort Bragg, North Carolina for five weeks of advisor training. Colin also was informed that he would be promoted to captain before he was shipped. The assignment was going to be for one year. Alma wanted to know what this meant for their relationship. All Colin could say was that you can write me and we will see what happens in the year. Alma said, "*I am not going to write you. If all we are going to be is pen pals, let's end it now.*" Colin was shocked by her response, and he drove back to Fort Devens heartbroken. After thinking that night, he realized that there was only one thing to do. He was going to ask Alma to marry him. He did not want to live without her.

Colin and Alma were married before he had to report to Fort Bragg for training. At the end of the five weeks, and Alma secure with her parents in Alabama, Colin shipped off for Saigon, arriving Christmas morning 1962. The Army had converted a posh hotel over to a bachelor barracks for foreign military advisors. The accommodations were definitely much nicer than Colin had expected. But the sweltering heat somewhat diminished the Christmas cheer.

Within a few days, Colin was placed with a Vietnamese combat unit, expected to advise them on how to stop the Viet Cong from making intrusions into the South Vietnam territories. The jungles had justified the army having the rangers train in the swamps and everglades of Florida. The physical demands of the daily marches validated those long training days. During the seven months that Colin was with the combat unit, they had gotten into numerous gun battles; had lost seven men and had another twenty-six injured. Colin was number twenty-seven and his minor lacerations marked the end of his tour with the unit. He had become basically unit commander, and felt very close to the men of this 2nd battalion, but because of their deployment he was unable to communicate with the unit during his recovery. Colin left the unit with great apprehension and remorse, worrying openly about their safety and regretting that he had to leave them.

Although Colin witnessed firsthand that this war could lead to an unimaginable number of causalities, he held steadfast to the conviction that the United States should help the South Vietnamese defend their independence. The South Vietnamese people wanted to be free of the communist dictators of the north; free to decide their fate and determine their own destiny. The war to maintain this freedom was going to take many more troops than the Americans were willing to commit. It was clear to Colin that America's involvement was grossly underestimated from the very start. When asked by an analyst in a intelligence briefing Colin without hesitation said, *"It'll take half a million men to succeed."*

Colin's opinion was of no concern to the army, and their involvement in Vietnam would continue on this partial basis, with no escalation necessary. The chain of command was confident that they could accomplish their objectives with this continued limited engagement. Information they were receiving from most field officers was skewed to provide the rosiest picture possible. As he had seen in Germany, self-delusion and misinformation was acute throughout the command structure.

With Colin's tour coming to an end, he was ready to leave Vietnam and return state side to see his new bride. Upon his arrival, there was just one person waiting to greet him. She seemed like a stranger, having not seen her in almost a year. But as soon as he held her in his arms, all the feeling which he had put aside came pulsating through his veins. They hurried to her parent's house where his real surprise was waiting. While he was wading through the swamps and jungles of Vietnam, Alma had given birth to their first child, Mike. Colin was a new daddy. He was not longer the bachelor or the married man in name only; he was now a family man, a husband and father.

With these new responsibilities in tow, Colin received his next assignment to report to Fort Benning and take career training classes in infantry and military tactics. The army was now going to teach Colin how to observe combat from the perspective of a decision maker. He was going to understand the deployment of troops from the logistical point of view. All that he knew to this moment was to follow orders without deviation or question.

Being again stationed in the south was going to be a challenge. He had to, as the colonel had suggest years ago, assume the posture of the *"good Negro."* He had gotten used to being overseas and having the ability to go anywhere he liked. But times were changing; the Congress was about to pass a civil rights bill banning segregation and discrimination on the basis of color. A few of Colin's classmates were debating the merits of the bill. The primary objection as one classmate argued, was not prejudice, but an issue of property rights; if someone opens a business, should they not have the right to serve who they wish? Colin could no longer constrain himself. He chimed in, *"If you're a soldier and you're black, you'd better have a strong bladder, because you won't be stopping much between Washington D.C. and Fort Benning."* He went on to describe how as night was falling it was almost impossible to find a hotel for his wife and child, where they could stay and get a good night sleep. Furthermore, sheriffs, law officers and vigilantes were killing innocent kids as they helped innocent people stand up for their rights. Is that property rights? Colin had acquired an appreciation for those southern blacks who have been able to withstand this lifelong onslaught of racism and overcome the tyranny. Having come from a West Indian background, he did not, until his stint in the army, have a true understanding for all they had to endure.

Over the next few years, life was smooth and relaxing. Colin was promoted to Major and President Johnson was pushing civil rights laws through Congress, making life in the south much easier to tolerate. The Powell's second child, Linda, was born. The army had provided a continuous flow of training courses at places like Fort Leavenworth and also approved Colin to begin taking classes for an MBA at an outside college. Colin's career was flourishing. Then the orders came he was to return to Vietnam, since the war was escalating and getting out of control, as Colin predicted many years ago. Colin tried to prepare Alma for the possibility of him not coming home from Vietnam. Alma had known many widows of servicemen at Fort Benning, so she reluctantly acknowledged the chance of her never seeing Colin again.

This second tour in Vietnam was much different from the first. The quaint colonial capital had been replaced by an ad hoc military compound, with US military vehicles and equipment buzzing all through Saigon. Colin was assigned to a *"resurrected*

168

World War II 23rd Infantry Division" as the executive officer. His job was to make sure the fighting group had all the supplies it needed to stay in strong fighting shape. Colin's role as executive officer lasted only a brief time because of his picture in the *Army Times* newspaper. Major General Charles M. Gettys recognized Colin from the picture of graduates of Leavenworth and immediately ordered him to become his plans officer. This position was usually held by lieutenant colonels; Colin was the only major filling the post in the entire army. This was his great break. In an instant, Colin went from taking care of the supplies of 800 men to planning the logistical deployment of 18,000 men and equipment. General Gettys took an incredible chance on a major he did not even know, who he merely only saw in the newspaper and had graduated second in his planning class at Leavenworth.

When Colin left Vietnam the first time he predicted it would take a half a million men to get the job done. He was wrong. The army was already up the 550,000 and the end of the war was nowhere in sight. Colin finished the remainder of his tour on General Gettys' staff well out of harm's way. But the experience and exposure had been invaluable. Although he eventually relinquished the planning officer's position to the lieutenant colonel Gettys, Colin stayed on as his assistant and learned a great deal.

The Vietnam War for Colin was over and he returned to the states and began his political ascension up the command structure by receiving a coveted White House fellowship. Colin started to take classes for his MBA at George Washington University, and the Powell's bought their first house in the Virginia area. The fellowship position required Colin to work as a liaison between the Congress, the White House and the Pentagon. The Pentagon at the time had a lot to answer for because of the mismanaged Vietnam War. President Nixon appointed a commission to investigate why the war was so badly handled and the commission did not look outside the army.

Colin received his promotion to Lieutenant Colonel while in the fellowship and his career continued rising through the Ford, Carter and Reagan administrations. Under Reagan he took the role of National Security Adviser, which gave him a direct line to the president. Colin admired President Reagan, which strongly influenced his later decision to become a republican. He finally reached the top military post under President George H. W. Bush which was Chairman of the Joint Chiefs of Staff. He stayed on under President Clinton to help provide a smooth transition. Then he accepted the position of Secretary of State under President George W. Bush. As he assumed all these different posts and positions, Colin Powell blazed the trail by being the first black man to hold most of these jobs. He did not lead a movement or participate in sit-ins; he simply persevered and overcame any obstacle which was placed in his way. With every subsequent appointment his visibility to the American people became more and more prominent; as a result, he created a conduit for blacks to attain greater heights.

Secretary Powell's footsteps have created the trail which has led to the election of the first black president, Barack Hussein Obama. President Obama should be the signal that the path is now permanently forged for all ethnicities and races. He, hopefully, indicates that regardless of your background any American can reach the *mountaintop*. His achievement opens the door to a new generation of Americans to take control of our future.

Although many want to believe that President Obama is African American, his father was directly from Kenya, and not a black person with American slave ancestry. President Obama's ethnicity is better characterized as half Kenyan-American. President Obama's story is uniquely American because he really did not know his father, so his Kenyan cultural identity was limited to the few times they corresponded in his life. He was raised primarily by his mother and her parents, leaving him with a missing part of his identity in a country which immediately, whether someone likes it or not, identifies a child of any mix as black, as the slave masters did a hundred years before. He spent most of his formative years among white people in Hawaii, who he related to culturally and socially but found he was still considered an outcast for no other reason than the color of his skin, resulting in confusion and bewilderment. Asking himself the question, *"How could I perform just as well or better than those kids, and still be seen as less?"* The same question most black Americans ask themselves at some moment in their lives.

Barack Hussein Obama, Jr. was born August 4, 1961 at Kapi'olani Medical Center in Honolulu, not far from Waikiki. On his birth certificate his mother's race is Caucasian and his father's is African, which obviously is not a race at all, so his confusion started from the beginning. The young parents got married to the dismay of both sides of the family. Barack Sr.'s father, Hussein Onyango Obama, wrote to his son that he disapproved of the marriage because this white woman would tarnish the Obama bloodline. Stanley Dunham, Ann's father, was also not thrilled that his young daughter was marrying so early and having a child, but he tried to support the couple anyway he could. At first, he disliked the relationship between his daughter and this black college student; however, he was quickly won over by the charm and intelligence of this truly gifted young man.

Barack Sr. was an economics student who was able to graduate the University of Hawaii in less than three years, receiving one of the top grades in his class. He was planning to attend graduate school and receive his PhD in Economics. He had the choice to stay in Hawaii, attend a New School in New York or attend Harvard. With no hesitation, Barack Sr. knew his only option was to go to the most prestigious school in the country. The only drawback was that he would be unable to afford to support his new family at Harvard. If he had chosen to accept the offer in New York, the school would have provided him a stipend

172

large enough to maintain his family. In 1963, Barack Sr. left for Harvard and was not seen by the family for another ten years. Barack wrote him on and off, but was never consistent. Ann filed for divorce in 1964, and Barack Sr. signed the papers without protest, when they were delivered to him in Cambridge. Years later an aunt from Kenya called Barack to tell him that Barack Sr. had died in a car accident.

Ann Dunham, in the absence of Barack's father, was the largest influence in his life. After Barack was born she decided to drop out of school and stay home with her infant in order to care for his needs. This was contrary to her personality, but she felt her child deserved the loving attention. Ann was an incredibly intelligent person in her own right. She had a passion for economics and anthropology. This was why she fell in love with Barack Sr. in the first place. When Barack Sr. left, and with the help of her parents, Ann enrolled in school at the University of Washington and took Barry, as she called him, with her to Seattle. It was obvious very early in Barry's life that Ann liked to move; she never really wanted to stay anywhere too long.

It did not take Ann long to realize that going to class, studying and taking care of a child was very difficult to do alone. After her first year at Washington, she moved back to Honolulu with her parents, so they could help her care for Barry. Stanley and Madelyn assumed many of the parental duties, while Ann studied for her degree. Barry called them Gramps and Toot. Gramps would take little Barack everywhere with him, and when people would stare at the mixed child he would approach them and strike up a conversation, pointing out that Barry was a member of the Hawaiian royal family. The Dunham's had instilled in their children many years ago that prejudice was wrong and everyone must be judged by their actions.

Ann met a new love interest. He was an Indonesian geologist studying for his Master's degree at the University. After dating for a while, Ann introduced Lolo Soertoro, to the whole family including Barry. Lolo was a much milder mannered individual than Barack Sr. Gramps liked that he was more *modest, less aggressive and far less ambitious,* and he would play chess for hours with him. Lolo was also good with Barack, allowing him to wrestle until his heart was content.

Lolo and Ann dated for two years while Ann finished her degree and Lolo completed his. By the time Barry was six years old, Ann sat him down and explained that Lolo had asked her to marry him, but Lolo had to return to Indonesia. As a result, they were going to move with Lolo. Barry liked Lolo and was quite accustomed to moving so he did not really object. Lolo left almost immediately since the Indonesian government called all students back to the country in order to help with the social unrest. It took Ann and Barry a few months to get passports and all the shots necessary to make the trip. In the mean time, Lolo was preparing for his new family with a house and a job to support his arrivals.

Ann and Barry landed in Jakarta, where Lolo met them with a smile. He had gained a few pounds and grown a mustache. Lolo whisked them past customs and into a waiting car. As they drove, Barry steered out the window to see strange animals roaming the streets. Lolo proclaimed that he had a surprise for Barry. Lolo drove up to their new house and a large hairy animal jumped out of a tree. There was an ape, named Tata, he brought back from New Guinea. Handing Barry a peanut from his pockets, he showed Barry how to feed his new pet. That night, as he lay in bed underneath his mosquito netting, Barry thought to himself that he truly had everything a boy could want.

Life over the next three years was one adventure after another for Barry. Lolo saw to it that Barry learned to fight when the older boys next door picked on him; he brought home boxing gloves. Any question Barry had about life, Lolo was there to explain in great detail in a way Barry could understand. He introduced Barry as his son but did not make him do anything he did not want to do. Lolo tried very hard to help Barry assimilate into the Indonesian society.

Ann never wanted Barry to forget he was American. Since she could not afford to send him to the school other Americans attended, she supplemented Barry's education with a correspondence course from the States. She would come into his room at four in the morning and make him do his three hour English lesson. This happened five days a week. Ann was determined that her son would not fall behind. Barry hated this regiment; however, that did not matter to Ann. She would simply say, *"This is no picnic for me either, buster."*

But Barry started to notice that Ann and Lolo were drifting apart, and he recognized that his mom seemed lonely and on edge. Lolo was never the same after returning to Indonesia. Ann would ask Lolo what was the matter, but Lolo would only respond that she would not understand. Within the last year, as their relationship was falling apart, Ann gave birth to Maya. Lolo treated Ann respectfully, but Ann was ready to leave and return to Hawaii. She could no longer take the loneliness and separation from her family. In addition, her hunger for studying anthropology and economics was growing. Ann felt completely unsatisfied.

She decided to send her ten year old son home to her parents. Ann could no longer keep up the early morning schedule, but would not let Barry fall behind in these Indonesian schools. Gramps and Toot were waiting for Barry as he exited the plane. At first he really did not recognize his grandparents, but quickly all his memories of the time he spent with them came rushing back. They had move from their home and was now living in a two bedroom apartment. Gramps' job as an insurance salesman was not going so well, but Toot was doing very well at the bank, which caused some friction in the household.

Gramps had signed Barry up for an elite private school that he had attended called Punahou. At that moment, Barry knew he was not going back to Indonesia to live with his mother and sister. Gramps was much more excited than Barry about the upcoming year at this new school. On their campus visit Gramps was beaming with excitement as they toured the pool, the gym and the lecture halls. Gramps said to Barry, is this not like heaven? Barry actually dreaded having to meet new friends and get use to a whole new system. He also missed his mother; Barry and Ann were very close and he hated being so far away from her.

Barry's first day at Punahou was, as he expected, awful. The other kids had laughed when they announced his name over the intercom, poking fun at the kid with the funny name. Most of the student had known each other since kindergarten and all lived in the same ritzy neighborhood. He did meet a great teacher named Miss Hefty. She greeted him on his first day with a pleasant smile. Miss Hefty told Barack that she used to live in Kenya and teach children in a village. He also met a shy black girl, named Joella Edwards, who before he arrived was the sole black person in their grade. From that first day they avoided each other as if their association would only further isolate the other.

The first month at Punahou was difficult for Barry. He was basically alone, cast away like he had some sort of disease. After a while, boys started to approach Barack and start conversation asking about his father. He slowly started making friends. Barack throughout the whole acclamation process was very confused as to why he was so ostracized, but he realized that he was no worse off than the many other students who for one reason or another also were categorized as misfits.

Suddenly, Barry's world would be shaken. Gramps and Toot received a telegram telling them that Barack Sr. would be paying them a visit two weeks after Ann was scheduled to arrive in Hawaii. Barry did not know how to respond. He was bewildered. Should he be excited? He was going to meet the father he had merely heard about. He was not sure what he had to do to prepare. Toot tried to fill his mind with facts pertaining to Kenya. Barack truly did not have any reaction on the news. He followed Toot's advice and went to the local library to get books on Kenya and the Luo tribe. Of course, there were very few books on the subject, merely a small paragraph in one of the encyclopedias.

The day finally came, and Ann and Maya had been in Hawaii for more than two weeks. Ann had set up a small apartment for Barack Sr. to stay while he recovered from injuries caused by a car accident. Ann had maintained contact with her first husband all the time she was in Indonesia. Barry met his father in the living room of his grandparents. Not knowing what to say he simply responded to his father's questions about school and life, never really divulging any deeper information. This superficial conversation went on for a month, either in the living room or on short walks around the University, while Barack Sr. recovered.

It all came to a climax; a few weeks before his father was to leave. Barry was watching TV, a Christmas special, and Barack Sr. sat down beside him to have their nightly chit chat.

When Barack Sr. felt Barry was not listening, he told him to go to his room and study. Gramps and Toot were angry that after all these years he came into their living room to reprimand Barry. Barack Sr. scolded them for spoiling the child, and allowing him to waste his time. Barry sat in his room listening to all the commotion and arguing. The next day Toot sent him to his father's apartment to deliver a message. Ann was there ironing Barack Sr. clothes. Barry was not sure whose side she was on. He raced out of the apartment as fast as he could. Within two weeks, he was gone, but his brief stay changed Barry forever.

Ann registered at the University to get her Master's in anthropology, and with her small stipend she was able to provide an apartment for Barry and Maya. For the next three years, Ann studied hard and so did Barry, getting mostly A's in his courses. Barry became obsessed with basketball, playing whenever he got a free moment. He got along with everyone at the school, seemed happy and well adjusted. Though below the surface Barry was having difficulties determining his own identity, caught between a white world which did not fully accept him, and a black world he did not really know. Barry could not relate to the struggles of the civil rights movement, but he knew he was discriminated against for being black, so where did he belong?

Ann had decided to pursue her doctorate in anthropology but she needed to go back to Indonesia to research her dissertation. When she told Barry, to her surprise he told her he would stay behind and finish his years at Punahou. He would simply move back in with Gramps and Toot, and live there until she returned. Barry had become comfortable living without Ann during all that time she was in Indonesia.

Ann and Maya returned to Indonesia and Barry moved back in with his grandparents. Barry gave an outward impression of a well adjusted, friendly, average high school student, but inside he constantly struggled with where he truly belonged. It did not matter how much he tried, he could never get fully accepted in the white world. However, as he watched TV and listened to music he could never completely relate to the black experience. He could not hate all white people or think they were devils; he did not live in the segregated south, so he could not appreciate the vile existence of being a second class citizen; he did not have generations before him who could relate stories of slavery and lynchings; and most importantly, he did not have any relatives who could demonstrate what it truly meant to be black. What he did have was the entire outside world calling him black and his immediate inner world being mostly white. Which world could he choose? Did he really have a choice when the world outside already labeled him?

These questions, and his confusion, started to impact Barry's studies. His grades started to slip, and he was afraid of being alone with no choices at all if he left Hawaii. As a result, he was not doing his college applications, either. Ann had no patience for this behavior. She confronted Barry on the issue, and demanded to know why he was being so lackadaisical with his future. She told him he could get into any school he wanted. Staying in Hawaii, or being like Gramps and not going to school were not options, neither would fulfill his destiny.

Punahou was renowned for sending its graduates to very prestigious schools all over the country, so the range of schools to which Barry could apply were vast. He began applying to many different schools, but ended up choosing Occidental College in California, near Pasadena. Occidental was a small school with only 1600 students, mostly middle and upper class families from California. Barry received financial aid, and by the end of high school had gotten a case of *"rock fever,"* a burning desire to leave Hawaii.

Barry excitedly started his career college career at Occidental. The school was incredibly diverse for only having 1600 students. Obama, which is what he now wanted to be called, quickly made friends, and his circle was very multiracial. It consisted mostly of Asian kids from Pakistan and India. In the school overall, there were seventy five black students who mostly kept to themselves. They basically created their own form of segregation, sitting at tables that were primarily all black, and seeking out only other black students. The black students seemed to try and keep everyone else out of the inner circle. Obama moved very smoothly between all the groups. He joined the black student association, but was not an overly active member; he associated with white students who were curious about his

Kenyan roots; and he kept his close multicultural friends who he related to the most.

Academically, Occidental did not provide nourishment for his ever growing appetite for larger, more important social issues. He wanted to understand the condition of African Americans, and black Americans in general. The small size of Occidental was great for learning about his inner person but it did not enable him to expand his mind and grasp the bigger issues which were plaguing the nation. He knew he needed to be in an urban area like New York, where he could be around more black people and comprehend their struggle. Obama was embarking on his own *Great Migration*, which so many blacks pursued in the 1920's and 40's. Like those young southern blacks, he wanted to go to Harlem and engage in the cultural renaissance of the time.

Obama, now more mature and surer of himself, applied for a transfer to Columbia University in New York City. In the summer, prior to enrolling at Columbia, Barack, the name he currently went by, took a trip to Asia to see his friends in Pakistan and India, and also visit Indonesia to see his mother and Maya. Being an adult gave him a completely different perspective of the rampant poverty which confronted him in each of these countries. As a child, he was not aware of the poverty the natives of these countries were facing, but with a new found understanding, he was devastated be the conditions that such a large number of people in the world had to live under. Later in his life, he speaks of this time as a changing moment where he starts to fully recognize the enormity of the problems facing the world.

At Columbia, Barack decided to *"buckle down"* and focus on his academics. He decided to stop partying, drinking, and youthful experimentation. He could not give up cigarettes, though he tried numerous times. Barack majored in political science with special emphasis on foreign policy, social issues, political theory and American history. Without all the partying, he spent his spare time going to political speeches in Harlem and attending different churches in the city. Barack was determined to clean up his act and make an impact on the world.

Columbia and New York were exactly what Barack hoped they would be when he left Occidental. They exposed him to the greater world where he could experience and learn about the bigger issues that were plaguing this nation and the world. Barack was caught dreaming of what he could do to fix the problems, while still being simply a college student. As a result, he tried to live as if he were suffering, depriving himself of simple pleasures as he could, so he would fully appreciate the tribulations of others.

On November 24, 1982, Barack found out that his father had died in a car accident after a night of drinking. Barack had reestablished some correspondence with his father, writing him an occasional letter in order to find out how his brothers and sisters were doing, and telling him how he was faring. But Barack had long ago decided to exclude from his identity, the man who chosen not to be part of his life. From that day in Hawaii, Barack could never again see his father as anything more than a far away image, never getting close enough to touch. Barack spoke to his mother concerning the death, but also since that day, he knew his mother envisioned his father through the rosy colored glasses of an eighteen year old in love. Barack did not attend the funeral, sending only a letter of condolence to his family from Kenya, wishing them well and holding out an olive branch for future contact. It was only after a dream that Barack finally acknowledged the influence his father had on him. He had always been just trying to reconcile why his father did not want to be with him. Barack tried to live up to the image he conjured in his mind of what his father wanted him to be.

With Columbia coming to an end, most of Barack's classmates were applying to law schools, other graduate institutions, or training programs. Barack decided he wanted to become a community organizer. He believed he could make a difference in these urban areas; however, all the letters he wrote to these charitable organization sponsoring workers went unopened. He needed money so he took a job writing reports on third world countries for a consulting firm. Although the reports were mainly for multi-national corporations wanting to enter a third world markets, he learned a great deal about the realities of international finance.

This employment was short lived; Barack never had the heart for writing reports for corporations. He took a position with a non-profit as an organizer. The organization was started with the help of Ralph Nader. The New York Public Interest Research Group exposed Barack to mobilizing college students to speak out on various issues. He also led a student campaign to Washington so they could lobby the New York delegation to oppose any cuts in student aid. After delivering a petition with thousands of names to the delegation, Barack and the students walked around to city to admire the buildings and the historical significant of the capitol. He was most fascinated with the White House, and how it sat so close to the street.

At the end of a year, Barack decided that he wanted to see another urban area in America. Through a mutual friend, Barack was able to get an organizer position at a new non-profit in Chicago. He was very excited and packed his car and drove to the windy city. He had been to Chicago one summer some fourteen years ago when Gramps took him on a trip to see his roots in the Midwest. Chicago was an extremely popular destination for young blacks during the Great Migration early in this century. Barack was just following in the footsteps of those mobile black Americans. The city had just elected it first black mayor, Harold Washington, and was in the forefront of racial integration. This was the perfect metropolis for an upwardly mobile black college graduate.

From the very beginning, Barack loved Chicago, but community organizing was a series of failures with a few infrequent successes. Barack struggled to keep his faith in the system and the people. He met all different types of people from many distinct ethnic backgrounds and numerous walks of life. He found solace in the teachers who wanted to change the world and cared so deeply in the mission they were trying to accomplish that it would inspire anyone to go out help them achieve their cause. He also was dragged down by those who saw no hope and could not bear to encounter the next negative occurrence in their lives. Barack met with church leaders who were struggling to keep their congregations together. They told Barack their fears and their frustrations.

Every church and each preacher Barack met inspired his desire to understand his own faith. Invariably, Barack would be asked, about his faith, and to this question he could only provide an indefinite answer. Ann was never a strong proponent of religion, although she did consider herself spiritual, and would urge the children to read the Bible. She gave Barack no guidance with respect to any particular religious group; hence, he was left to find his own path. Barack performed a thoughtful search speaking to many different preachers and ministers until one was able to move him. Jeremiah Wright, pastor of the Trinity Church, a large black congregation in the south end of the city, connected on a spiritual level with Barack, assuming the function of a religious mentor. Reverend Wright, however, was very controversial in his views, advocating black liberation and empowerment, emphasizing the differences that he believed was inherent between the races. For some one seeking a strong black role model, Reverend Wright was a lightning rod.

This time in Chicago as a community organizer lasted almost three years, before Barack was overcome with the burning desire to do more with his life and earn more money so he could someday support a family. Barack reasoned that a law degree would achieve both goals, and like his father, there was only one school in the country for him to attend and that was Harvard Law.

As Barack was leaving Chicago, Mayor Harold Washington died at his desk after being reelected to another term the year before. Barack was very fond of the mayor. He had met him a few times and thought that Washington had done a great job lifting himself to the office of mayor, but had done a lousy job creating a lineage of black politicians which could follow in his footsteps. Mayor Washington had centered everything around one person, not taking into consideration the greater cause. Thus, after his death, the fate of many black politicians in the city died with him.

Although he had learned a great deal about community organizing and building a campaign from the ground up, he was ready for a new challenge. After talking to his Kenyan brothers, he realized that his father, in the last year of his life, was disheartened by his missed possibilities. He was angry that he had never gotten the opportunity to fulfill his great potential. Barack Sr. felt trapped by his obligation to his country and his people, never being able to fully achieve all the promise he saw in himself. Barack wanted to make sure this would not happen to him. He was going to quest for greatness, in no way overlooking the opportunity to reach for the stars. Harvard Law provided him this chance.

In the fall of 1988, Barack Obama enrolled in Harvard Law School. He was sure that Harvard would teach him a different *"way of thinking."* Harvard would be that challenging environment Barack was seeking. The faculty and the students would demand the best of Barack, allowing him to leave nothing on the court but his most outstanding performance. Barack was no longer the young confused kid that graduated Punahou; the years had created a confident man who knew he wanted to change the world and aspire to do his very finest work.

Barack distinguished himself through his mature manner and worldly intellect. He focused all his attention on attaining his goals, and pushing forward to learn as much as he could. It was always understood that Barack was on an intellectual crusade, which would end with him entering public life and making a difference in the nation and the world. Barack was sometimes ridiculed for his constant need for consensus; he wanted to leave no one behind when a decision had to be made. Barack was, above all, a liberal intellectual seeking grand solutions to perplexing problems.

Harvard was a whirlwind tour that flew by very quickly. Barack was able to absorb incredible amounts of knowledge as he passed through the halls. The climax to his career at Harvard came when he was named President of the *Law Review*. He served on the *Law Review* for a year before he became president.

188

This appointment made him the first black president of the *Law Review*. His uncanny ability to smoothly transition between any group gave him an advantage over other students. Barack had been active in the black students association as well as among faculty members. He related to white students just as easily as he engaged with blacks. Barack's racially unique past made him a conduit capable of joining all groups together.

With his law degree, Barack returned to Chicago and took a position with a civil rights law firm. However, he was quickly recruited to organize a voter's registration drive in African American and Hispanic communities called *Project Vote*. The aim was to help stem the tide of republican dismantling of the social safety net started under Reagan. In this role, Barack had to call on government officials for their support and cooperation in motivating their constituents to come out and vote. The exposure *Project Vote* gave Barack was invaluable. Everyone in the city with any political influence was a target of the project, so they became familiar with Barack Obama. It was also obvious that this organizer was going to be a future extraordinary politician and leader.

The forthcoming course of Barack Obama was established in these days as a community organizer. No one could have predicted the speed of his ascension after this project, but it was clear that he would someday attain the pinnacle of his endeavors. Barack was literally and figuratively a shooting star, where the alignment of the universe allowed him to reach the office of

President of the United States. Barack has set the stage for the next great leader whose story has yet to be told. Someone with a background which will uniquely prepare him/her for the obstacles that lies ahead. Barack, like those before him, constructed a foundation which, if properly encouraged, will be able to support the development of generations to come. President Obama exemplifies that black Americans may have to wait a little bit longer, but that wait will not be fruitless. The *mountaintop* is within sight, and Dr. King will watch proudly from above as future children reach where he could not lead us, because others have taken the mantle and created a path to the *Promised Land*.

All I have learned

Resolution of this struggle represents the unrealized conclusion of Dr. King's mission and the fulfillment of our founding fathers' creation. As Dr. King articulated in numerous speeches over and over again, *the civil rights movement is greater than any one person and must continue until all black children are seen for the content of their character not judged merely by the color of their skin.* Today, in our ever more diverse society, we can expand that vision to include all our children. Through legislation and court orders, we have established much of the framework to regulate discriminating behavior; now we are all obligated to educate ourselves with respect to the dilemmas of African Americans as they quest to achieve equality. Because only through their accomplishment will the rest of us black, brown, yellow, and even white people who also love this country, be able to come to America and achieve our rightful portion of the *American Dream.* If any group is denied the ability to acquire their dream, then we are all vulnerable, and America shall never realize the promise our forefathers bestowed upon us.

America was never a place for the privileged few; it is a land for the many who wish to achieve their dreams, while overcoming the trials and tribulations, which everyone claims builds character, as we muddle through. Life is difficult enough and indiscriminately unfair without those who deliberately place artificial barriers in our path. Our founding fathers envisioned a country that in order to establish a *more perfect union* consistently strived to allow its citizens to embrace their lives, relish in their liberty and pursue their happiness. They reasoned that the only way to see this vision come true was to live and govern by the creed that "*All men are created equal.*"

When we deviate from this elementary formula and try to diminish the value of our creed by not living up to its simple notion, we tear our union apart. The Civil War was that moment in our history where we had to defend this basic idea which invariably made our nation so great. We can never forget all the lives that were lost attempting to secure life, liberty and the pursuit of happiness for all those who came after. Their sacrifices are what enable our children to prosper today. America's willingness to stand up and fight for the rights of each citizen is the reason our democracy will thrive well into the future.

The grand experiment can only fail if those few citizens who are ignorant of our past and afraid for their futures continue to fan the flames of the residual anger and resentment that too many still harbor towards people of different colors or backgrounds. It is evident that these groups were used by some to limit the rights and actions of others. But it was not their construct which perpetuated these violations of civil liberties; consequently, they cannot forever be held responsible for the misguided deeds of an overzealous few. We must get past our false belief that the successes of one group destine another group to failure. America has never been a *zero sum gain*. The achievements of any group has always been a source of power for the nation as a whole, so to believe that we will now collapse because African Americans or Hispanics get to exercise their rights is merely encouraging unsubstantiated fears of a fictitious America.

Our Constitution is based on the inflow of immigrants who for the last two hundred and thirty seven years have built and strengthened our Union. Our growth was the result of all the differences of each group coming together to forge an unbreakable, diverse society with a common core of liberty. It was not based on the notion that white people govern better or black people are not deserving of a chance; it was construed on the premise that all people must be given an equal opportunity to make their own way, and not held back because of extraneous values like birth right, religious affiliation or where a person comes from. The greatness of our Constitution is not solely in what it contains; it is also what the founding fathers chose to leave out. It does not say that whites are better, so they must lead; it does not outline that the richer someone is, the smarter they are, so they must lead; nor does it transcribe that Christians are greater than all other religious groups, so they must lead. It simply says, *"We the People…"*

We are all a product of their construction, and as such are entitled to express a voice in the development of this nation. But that message should not be used to silence the voices of others as they try to be heard, regardless of whether their opinion differs from our own. Everyone has something to contribute to the growth of our democracy. African Americans, as history demonstrates, have arduously toiled in the establishment of this great nation. They have fought in wars to defend our national freedoms; they have performed in sporting events to show our national pride; they have labored in jobs to expand our national infrastructure; and they have slaved to enhance our national wealth. African Americans have demonstrated their worth beyond any group in our nation's history, and still they must struggle for true equality. As I illustrated throughout this book, advancements have been made and progress will continue to move us forward, but it is each citizen's responsibility to insure our creed applies to all men.

Dr. King, in his book <u>Why We Can't Wait,</u> articulated the urgency of the moment, and how it is in the best interest of the nation to foster the process of equality through the heartlands of America.

> The Negro in winning rights for himself produces substantial benefits for the nation. Just as a doctor will occasionally reopen a wound, because a dangerous infection hovers beneath the half-healed surface, the revolution for human rights is opening up unhealthy areas in American life and permitting a new and wholesome healing to take place. Eventually the civil rights movement will have contributed infinitely more to the nation than the eradication of racial injustice. It will have enlarged the concept of brotherhood to a vision of total interrelatedness.

His message was relevant then, and is even more pertinent today. As our nation matures into the twenty-first century, we will face changes and new realities which shall challenge our national resolve, not from enemies outside, but from citizens who question the validity of the platform which our founders established. It is the American way to examine even our most closely held values. However, when we tarnish those principles solely on the basis that we are afraid to allow others to utilize them then we are not thoughtfully reaffirming our rights, we are destroying our nation.

I believe I am uniquely positioned to speak on the importance of maintaining steadfast to our values and principles. Being a black immigrant affords me the ability to analyze the aspects of our nation which has allowed it to flourish for two centuries. In addition, being from a nation that cannot achieve a harmonious existence because its system rewards citizens disproportionately based on characteristics such as who someone knows or how much they will pay, provides me with the perspective and knowledge to fully embrace and appreciate what America champions and defends.

Although like many black Americans throughout history, I too have questioned whether this unwavering loyalty is justified, when someone seemingly cleans every aisle I walk in while I am shopping in a store; when someone walks on the other side of the street on a dark night because they see me coming; when someone locks themselves in their car as I walk by; when someone emphasizes at a job interview the importance of not stealing and being punctual; or when someone does not find it necessary to protect a seventeen year old black child against a twenty eight year old man. For these reasons, I sometimes doubt my trust in the system, but quickly I remember, as the black soldiers did in World War I and World War II, America is a growing, evolving nation moving ever closer to its *more perfect union*. Through the perseverance of our amazing citizens, we will achieve the ideals set forth by our founders. Subsequently, every day I meet fellow Americans in all walks of life who reinvigorate my conviction.

It was because of this confidence in our nation and its people that Dr. King could prophetically proclaim in his "*I have a Dream*" speech on August 28, 1963 at the March on Washington. *With this faith we will be able to transform the jangling discords of our nation into a beautiful symphony of brotherhood. With this faith we will be able to work together, to pray together to struggle together, to go to jail together, to stand up for freedom together, knowing that we will be free one day....This will be the day, this will be the day when all of God's children will be able to sing with new meaning: "My country 'tis of thee, sweet land of liberty, of thee I sing. Land where my fathers' died, land of the Pilgrim's pride, from every mountainside, let freedom ring!" And if America is to be a great nation, this must become true.*

Bibliography

1. Carson, Clayborne, ed. *The Autobiography of Martin Luther King, Jr.* New York: Intellectual Properties Management, Inc. 1998.

2. King Jr., Martin Luther, *Why we can't wait.* New York: New American Library. 1963.

3. Obama, Barack, *Dreams from my father.* New York: Three Rivers Press. 1995.

4. Muhammad, Elijah, *Message to the Blackman in America.* Phoenix: Secretarius MEMPS Publications. 1965.

5. Washington, Denzel, *A Hand to Guide Me.* Des Moines: Meredith Books. 2006.

6. McWhorter, John, *Losing the Race: Self-sabotage in Black America.* New York: HarperCollins Publishers Inc. 2000.

7. Williams, Juan, *Enough.* New York: Crown Publishers. 2006.

8. Clark, Reginald M., *Family Life and School Achievement.* Chicago: University of Chicago Press. 1983.

9. Mosley, Walter ed., *Black Genius: African American solutions to African American problems.* New York: W.W. Norton & Company. 1999.

10. Haley, Alex ed., *The Autobiography of Malcolm X.* New York: Random House Publishing Group. 1964.

11. Yinger, John, *Closed Doors, Opportunities Lost: the continuing costs of housing discrimination.* New York: Russell Sage Foundation. 1995.

12. Wilson, William Julius, *When Work Disappears*. New York: Alfred A Knopf. 1996.

13. Dyson, Michael Eric, *Is Bill Cosby Right?*. New York: Basic Civitas Books. 2005.

14. Halberstam, David, *War in a Time of Peace*. New York: Touchstone Books. 2001.

15. Hauser, Thomas, *Muhammad Ali: His Life and Times*. New York: Touchstone Books. 1991.

16. Garvey, Marcus, *Selected Writings and Speeches of Marcus Garvey*. Mineola: Dover Publishing, Inc. 2004.

17. Ginsburg, Helen ed., *Poverty, Economics and Society*. Boston: Little, Brown and Company. 1972.

18. Friedman, Milton, *Capitalism and Freedom*. Chicago: University of Chicago Press. 1962.

19. Douglass, Frederick, *Narrative of the Life of Frederick Douglass: An American Slave*. New York: New American Library. 1997.

20. Axelrod, Alan, *The Life and Work of Thomas Jefferson*. Indianapolis: Alpha Books. 2001.

21. Rossiter, Clinton ed., *The Federalists Papers: Hamilton. Madison. Jay*. New York: Penguin Books USA. 1961.

22. Adler, Bill ed., *America's Founding Fathers: Their uncommon wisdom and wit*. Lanham: Taylor Trade Publishing. 2005.

23. Boskin, Michael J., *Reagan and the Economy*. San Francisco: Institute of Contemporary Studies. 1989.

24. Smiley, Tavis ed., *The Covenant with Black America.* Chicago: Third World Press. 2006.

25. Black, Conrad, *Franklin Delano Roosevelt: Champion of Freedom.* New York: Public Affairs. 2003.

26. Halberstam, David, *The Children.* New York: Random House Publishing Group. 1998.

27. Halberstam, David, *The Best and The Brightest.* New York: Ballantine Books. 1969.

28. Barton, David, George Washington, "*Thomas Jefferson and Slavery in Virginia.*" Wallbuilders.com. January 2000. <http://www.wallbuilders.com/LIBissuesArticles.asp?id=99>

29. "*Slavery and the Making of America,*" Public Broadcast Network. Thirteen/WNET New York. 2004. <http://www.pbs.org/wnet/slavery/about/index.html>

30. Ambrose, Stephen, "*Jim Crow and Black Soldiers.*" *Citizen Soldier.* New York: Simon & Schuster. 1997. <http://www.worldwar2history.info/Army/Jim-Crow.html>

31. Duncan, Melba J., "*Current Challenges in the African-American Community,*" *The Complete Idiot's Guide to African-American History.* New York: Penguin Books USA. 2003. <http://school.familyeducation.com/african-american-history/race/47078.html?page=1>

32. "*African American contemporary issues,*" Wikibin.org <http://wikibin.org/articles/african-american-contemporary-issues.html>

33. "*The Black Population: 2010,*" United States Census Bureau. September 2011.

<http://www.census.gov/prod/cen2010/briefs/c2010br-06.pdf>

34. *"The Moynihan Report (1965),"Blackpast.org.* March 1965.
    <http://www.blackpast.org/primary/moynihan-report-1965>

35. *"Census of Population and Housing,"* United States Census
    Bureau. 2011. <
    http://www.census.gov/prod/www/decennial.html>

36. *"Births: Final Data for 2010,"* National Vital Statistics
    Reports. Vol. 61, No. 1. August 2012.
    <http://www.cdc.gov/nchs/data/nvsr/nvsr61/nvsr61_01_tabl
    es.pdf#I04>

37. *"About The State of Working America." The State of
    Working America.* Economic Political Institute. 2012.
    <http://stateofworkingamerica.org/about/>

38. *"Unemployment rate of workers age 16 and older by race
    and ethnicity, 1973–2013," The State of Working America.*
    Economic Political Institute. 2012.
    <http://stateofworkingamerica.org/charts/unemployment-by-
    race-and-ethnicity/>

39. *"Child Outcomes and Classroom Quality in FACES 2009,"
    OPRE Report 2012-37a.* Office of Planning, Research and
    Evaluation. September 2012.
    <http://www.acf.hhs.gov/sites/default/files/opre/faces_2009.
    pdf>

40. Lake, Thomas, *"Did This Man Really Cut Michael
    Jordan?"SI Vault. Sports Illustrated.* January 16, 2012.
    *<http://sportsillustrated.cnn.com/vault/article/magazine/MA
    G1193740/1/index.htm>*

41. *"The Rise and Fall of Jim Crow Laws,"* Public Broadcast
    Network. Thirteen/WNET New York. 2002.
    <http://www.pbs.org/wnet/jimcrow/index.html>

42. Pilgrim, David, *"Who was Jim Crow?" Jim Crow Museum of Racist Memorabilia.* Ferris State University. Big Rapids. 2012. <http://ferris.edu/news/jimcrow/who.htm>

43. Burrell, Tom, *Brainwashed : Challenging the Myth of Black Inferiority.* Carlsbad: Smiley books. 2010.

44. Remnick, David, *The Bridge: the life and rise of Barack Obama.* New York: Alfred A. Knopf. 2010.

45. Jordan, Michael, *Driven from within / Michael Jordan; edited by Mark Vancil._* New York: Atria Books. 2005.

46. Powell, Colin L., *It worked for me: in life and leadership / Colin Powell with Tony Koltz.* New York: Harper. 2012.

47. Frady, Marshall, *Jesse : the life and pilgrimage of Jesse Jackson / Marshall Frady.* New York : Random House. 1996.

48. Powell, Colin L., *My American Journey / Colin L. Powell, with Joseph E. Persico.* New York : Random House. 1995.